Criminal
Law

LAW AND CRIMINAL JUSTICE SERIES
Series Editor: James A. Inciardi
Division of Criminal Justice, University of Delaware

The **Law and Criminal Justice Series** provides students in criminal justice, criminology, law, sociology, and related fields with a set of short textbooks on major topics and subareas of the field. The texts range from books that introduce the basic elements of criminal justice for lower-division under-graduates to more advanced topics of current interest for advanced under-graduates and beginning graduate students. Each text is concise, didactic, and produced in an inexpensive paperback as well as hardcover format. Each author addresses the major issues and areas of current concern in that topic area, reporting on and synthesizing major research done on the subject. Case examples, chapter summaries, and discussion questions are generally included in each volume to aid in classroom use. The modular format of the series provides attractive alternatives to large, expensive classroom textbooks and timely supplements to more traditional class materials.

Volumes in this series:

Additional volumes currently in development.

Criminal Law

Understanding Basic Principles

CHARLES W. THOMAS
DONNA M. BISHOP

Volume 8.
Law and Criminal Justice Series

SAGE PUBLICATIONS
The Publishers of Professional Social Science
Newbury Park   Beverly Hills   London   New Delhi

To Our Parents
Charles H. and Virgina P. Thomas
and
Joseph F. and Dorothy A. Bishop

For information address:

SAGE Publications, Inc.
2111 West Hillcrest Drive
Newbury Park, California 91320

SAGE Publications Inc.
275 South Beverly Drive
Beverly Hills
California 90212

SAGE Publications Ltd.
28 Banner Street
London EC1Y 8QE
England

SAGE PUBLICATIONS India Pvt. Ltd.
M-32 Market
Greater Kailash I
New Delhi 110 048 India

Printed in the United States of America

Library of Congress Cataloging-in-Publication Data

Main entry under title:

Thomas, Charles Wellington, 1943-
    Criminal law.

(Law and criminal justice series ; v. 8)
    Bibliography: p.
    Includes index.
    1. Criminal law—United States.   I. Bishop, Donna M.
II. Title. III. Series.
KF9219.T46   1986   345.73   85-30443
ISBN 0-8039-2668-5   347.305
ISBN 0-8039-2669-3 (pbk.)

FIRST PRINTING

CONTENTS

PREFACE

There was a time in the fairly recent history of American criminology when many if not most criminologists recognized that the demands of their discipline required a reasonably well-developed understanding of substantive criminal law and criminal procedure. Evidence of this may be found even in introductory criminology textbooks of the type authored by such figures as Richard A. Korn and Lloyd W. McCorkle (*Criminology and Penology*, published in 1959) and Paul W. Tappan (*Crime, Justice and Correction*, published in 1960). However, somewhere along the way—perhaps as American criminology came to be thoroughly dominated by persons whose training was largely in sociology and as sociology sought to elevate its status as a behavioral science discipline—we lost touch with the world of law. We came to think that law is the proper province of lawyers and of law professors and that the behavior of those who apply or who violate the law is the territory of criminology. Those working in the areas of criminal law and criminal procedure soon came to be of less and less relevance to criminologists. Criminologists, in turn, were perceived by those with special interests in law to be little more than part of that undifferentiated mass of people "on the other side of the campus" who were uninterested in and uninformed about law.

The lack of a firm linkage between law and criminology has never had the slightest rationale. During the past two decades or so, however, it has had many consequences that seem almost bizarre. A generation or two of criminologists, for instance, became so blissfully ignorant of the subject matter of law that they wrote and relied upon textbooks within which such terms as crime, delinquency, law, felony, misdemeanor, and many more were used but never given definitions. Similarly, one routinely encounters work by those trained in law as well as judicial opinions written by, to choose only the most obvious illustration, the members of the United States Supreme Court in which authors cry out for empirical evidence regarding various serious concerns like the effectiveness of alternative sentencing models, capital punishment, and the relative advantages of privately retained and publicly appointed counsel. They are apparently unaware of the considerable research literature that criminologists have produced on these and a host of other important legal issues.

The tide now seems to be changing. Criminologists increasingly are coming to think of themselves as people who share many interests with their sociological colleagues who specialize in the sociology of law and the sociology of deviance but who also are a "different breed." Whether they think of themselves as representatives of a fully independent discipline (which happens to be our view of ourselves) or as participants in an interdisciplinary enterprise, they understand the necessity of having a basic appreciation for relevant aspects of law (and also of anthropology, economics, history, philosophy, political science, and a good deal more). They recognize that they cannot "do criminology" in an adequately sophisticated manner if they persist in pretending that ignorance is a virtue when every shred of logic and evidence proves it to be a vice.

And what, one might well be asking, is the relevance of these comments to the discussion we are about to begin? The relevance is really quite simple. This is a book about basic principles of substantive criminal law—its history, its structure, its diverse and sometimes contradictory purposes, and its application. The book is written not by lawyers or law professors but by two criminologists that regularly and routinely confront undergraduate students who, although often planning careers that are not law-related, have a sincere interest in the subject matter of both substantive and procedural criminal law. The book is written to and for that audience—and also to those of our behavioral science colleagues who recognize how they, too, might profit from a review of fundamental legal theories, terms, and concepts.

We introduce what is to come with no more than a single but exceedingly important qualification: It is entirely impossible to identify anything beyond very general principles of criminal law in so concise a monograph. At quite literally dozens of points in our writing we have had to force ourselves away from a more exhaustive examination of the issues we had touched upon. We did so out of a feeling that the purposes of this book would best be served if we sacrificed depth of discussion in order to achieve the objective of an adequately broad scope of coverage. Hopefully, however, our frequent references to significant judicial opinions and related scholarly research will serve as an initial guide for those who wish to pursue various topics more thoroughly.

In any event, the discussion has been divided into six chapters. The first seeks to provide an overview of the history and development of law—especially those foundations for our system of criminal jurisprudence that are to be found in the English common law tradition. Attention then shifts to a reasonably detailed discussion of the characteristic features of criminal law, to an examination of the essential elements one finds in definitions of crimes, and to a brief overview of contemporary sources of criminal law. Chapter 3 is devoted to some very different concerns, for there we consider basic theories about the origins and uses of law as well as various models that have been put forward in an attempt to justify the imposition of punishment by the state. The next three chapters shift the focus of the discussion back to fundamental principles of substantive criminal law. More specifically, Chapter 4 identifies basic limitations on the forms of conduct that may be defined as crimes and some constitutionally-based limits on the state's efforts to prosecute. This basic theme continues in Chapter 5, for that chapter is devoted to many of the problems the state must overcome in its effort to claim jurisdiction over particular offenses and particular offenders. Finally, all of Chapter 6 reviews a sample of the most common justifications, defenses, and excuses defendants rely upon when they are charged with violations of criminal law.

ACKNOWLEDGMENTS

Whether it involves a modest or an unusually ambitious objective, writing is seldom an exciting activity. The seemingly endless hours one spends behind a desk—or in our case behind a microcomputer—are hours that are lost to friends, family, and other personal interests. And there is more to it all than some consideration of these sorts of losses. Those who occupy themselves with writing have a way of becoming so consumed with their subject matter that they tend to impose on everyone else with whom they come in contact by babbling about the topic they wrote about the previous day. Thus, they often deserve to be thought of as a pain in the posterior of everyone they know.

Here, fortunately, we have an opportunity to do three things. The first is to extend a formal apology to those who have tolerated our single-minded commitment to completing this work and our consequent inattention to their preferences. The second is to express our sincere thanks to those of our colleagues and students who have commented on draft versions of one or more of the following chapters. We are especially indebted to Alexis Durham and Lonn Lanza-Kaduce, two of our colleagues in the University of Florida's Center for Studies in Criminology and Law, and to Dianne Bolinger, one of the Center's secretaries who is recognized by all associated with it as the only person talented enough to inject some degree of order into what would otherwise be total chaos. In addition, the senior author is most appreciative of the input he received from an unusually gifted group of young law students who enrolled in a seminar he taught at the University of Florida's College of Law. More than a little of what appears here flows from the ability of those students to teach a criminologist more about criminal law than he may have been able to teach them about criminology.

Finally, perhaps one of the most meaningful and personal opportunities authors have is to dedicate the product of their labor to someone, often someone to whom they owe a debt that is larger than they will ever be able to pay. Each of us is in precisely such a position. It is with much love, gratitude, and respect that we dedicate this modest work to our parents, Charles H. Thomas, Sr., Virginia P. Thomas, Joseph F. Bishop, and Dorothy A. Bishop.

—*Charles W. Thomas*
Donna M. Bishop
Center for Studies in Criminology
and Law
University of Florida

1

THE HISTORY AND DEVELOPMENT OF LAW

We must begin our study with an obvious problem of definition. What is law? The question is deceptively simple. Law is such an integral aspect of our lives that we seldom pause to reflect on its meaning. When we do, we find that the concept is elusive. Philosophers, legal scholars, theologians, and social scientists have discussed and debated the issue for centuries. In fact, the eminent legal anthropologist E. Adamson Hoebel once remarked that, "To seek a definition of law is like the quest for the Holy Grail" (1954: 18).

We can begin to appreciate the formidability of the problem by considering the variety of meanings we attach to law in everyday life. To some of us law is thought of in terms of legal professionals and the things that they do. The law is the police officer on the street. It is the work of elected representatives who enact legislation. It is the work of attorneys who represent clients and of judges who render decisions. To others, law is a set of rules, commands, or directives. It is what requires the payment of taxes, prohibits the sale of marijuana, and threatens to deprive us of our liberty should we fail to do the one or proceed to do the other. It is what commands that children attend school, that workers receive at least a minimum wage, that public utilities charge reasonable rates, that automobiles meet certain safety standards, and what in hundreds of other ways affects almost every aspect of our lives. Many look at law from more lofty vantage points. To some of them law is a divinely inspired set of eternal and unalterable truths. To others law signifies our development of principles for living that have been derived from logic and experience. To still others, law is an exercise of raw force in the service of a variety of ends (for example, the reinforcement of customary modes of conduct, the engineering of social change, the imposition of a particular group's notion of morality on all of us, and the systematic oppression of the powerless by the powerful).

Fortunately, our definitional task is simplified by our purposes. We need not spell out the meaning of law in all its complexity. It will suffice if we can arrive at a working definition that marks the broad contours of what we mean by law. We can begin with the simple observation that rules are essential to orderly social existence. Without rules to produce patterned modes of conduct, social life would soon degenerate into chaos. Law is an important part of this regulatory system. It is one of the means that societies employ to encourage desired modes of behavior. However, law is not adequately defined in these terms. There are many rules and accompanying sanctions that do not involve law. For example, parents often establish rules for their children whose violation may result in a spanking or loss of privileges. We might think of these rules as "laws" of the household, but that is not the ordinary sense in which we use the term law. Similarly, it is normative in our society that men wear trousers. If a man wears a dress, he may be subject to gossip, ridicule, ostracism, or other forms of social censure. Thus, we can have a rule backed by the threat of sanctions but still not have a violation of law. Something more formal is required before we define a norm as a law.

That "something more" has concerned scholars for centuries. One of the most well-known definitions is that offered by Benjamin Cardozo, who defined law as "a principle of conduct so established as to justify a prediction with reasonable certainty that it will be enforced by the courts if its authority is challenged" (1924: 52). Cardozo viewed enforcement by the court as the distinguishing feature of law. But what is a court? If the term means an official, organized tribunal with the specialized function of enforcing rules of conduct, then his definition is of limited utility. There are many primitive societies, for example, which are generally recognized as having had law but that lacked such adminis- trative bodies.

Others have offered definitions broad enough to encompass the law of primitive peoples. For example, an influential conception of law was provided by Max Weber. He defined law as "an order [that is] externally guaranteed by the probability that coercion (physical or psychological), to bring about conformity or avenge violation, will be applied by a *staff* of people holding themselves specially ready for that purpose" (1954: 5). This definition is superior to Cardozo's in at least two respects. First, it emphasizes the coercive nature of the law. Law is an order or a directive that has at least a reasonable probability of being backed by force. Second, through its reference to a specialized staff rather than a court, Weber's definition is applicable to law administered by, for example, ad hoc tribal councils that respond to rule violations among many primitive peoples. A similar definition is offered by the anthropologist Hoebel: "A social norm is legal if its neglect or infraction is regularly met, in threat or in fact, by the application of physical force by an individual or group possessing the socially recognized privilege of so acting" (1954: 28).

Both of these definitions include references to rules, sanctions, and to some body authorized to administer sanctions. Nevertheless, these definitions are not without shortcomings as well. Consider, for example, the cases of university students who are caught cheating on exams. They may be referred to a student court that is authorized to hear the matter and to impose sanctions. According to any of the above definitions, there has been a violation of a legal norm. However, we would not view students brought before such quasicourts as having broken the law. Consequently, our definition then must be amended to include reference to some political authority. It is the body of rules enacted and enforced by some sovereign political entity (a municipality, a state, a nation, a tribe) that we have in mind when we speak of law. Without belaboring the point any longer, we will define law as *a body of rules created by a political entity that is supported by the threat of sanctions to be imposed by authorized representatives of that political entity.*

ANCIENT LEGAL SYSTEMS

Law has been with us for thousands of years. Although a primary purpose of this chapter is to examine the development of our legal system, we will begin by noting important connections between contemporary and ancient legal systems.

The Law of Babylon

The first highly developed legal system of which we have record is that of ancient Babylon. Babylonian law strongly influenced the Roman law. Roman law, in turn, influenced Anglo-American law. Thus, at least a brief consideration of Babylonian law is appropriate here.

Much of what we know of the law of Babylon is contained in the Code of Hammurabi, written about 2100 B.C. It provided a detailed statement of the law and is thought by most historians to represent the reduction to written form of preexisting customs. Like other law givers in ancient times, Hammurabi is said to have attributed the code to the command of the god of the city: "He lived in that early age when all law was attributed to the gods, and when law was not yet completely split off from religion, and when the secular legislative, and the priestly revelatory, functions were not yet separated" (Kinnane, 1952: 175).

Nevertheless, it is important to note that, unlike most early systems of law—including the Hindu Code of Manu, the Egyptian law of Menes, and the Koran of the Moslem prophet Muhammed—the law of Babylon was compiled by a secular ruler.

A second feature of the Code of Hammurabi that is noteworthy is that it dealt with a variety of specialized matters (e.g., property, contracts, partnerships, sales, leases, mortgages, inheritance, crimes, and much more). That this was a remarkable achievement for its time should be evident from the fact that such topics were not addressed in English law until about 3000 years later.

Third, some attribute to the Code of Hammurabi the initial expression of the notion that law must be just (Kinnane, 1952: 177). Although the Code does not explicitly recognize that arbitrarily created and capriciously applied rules invite unrest, permeating the Code of Hammurabi is the theme that the law must be fair both in substance and in application. A clear attempt to translate an early conception of justice into practice is found in the Code's specification of a precise system of penalties for law violations that require offenses to be punished in proportion to the harm done. For example, the Code states that "if a man destroy the eye of another man, they shall destroy his eye," and "if a man knock out the tooth of a man of his own rank, they shall knock out his tooth" (Harper, 1904: 73, 75). The retaliatory principle reflected in this system of punishments is often called *lex talionis* or "in kind" retributivism. It is found in a modified form in many modern sentencing schemes that justify punishments in terms of "just dessert."

Finally, it is interesting to note that the Code of Hammurabi considered the social standing of the victim as a factor in determining the appropriate punishment. For example, if a man knocked out the tooth of a man of lower rank, he would merely pay a fine. However, he would lose his own tooth if he knocked out the tooth of a man of equal rank. Although most modern penal codes do not formally recognize the social standing of the victim as a proper consideration in sentencing, in the actual application of sentences such considerations sometimes do come into play. For example, in this country injuries to whites inflicted by blacks are often treated as more serious offenses than are injuries to blacks inflicted by whites (see, for example, Wolfgang and Reidel, 1973).

Mosaic Law

Probably no other system of law has had as great an influence on western civilization as Mosaic (Hebrew) law. Mosaic law is thought to have developed shortly after the exodus of the Israelites from Egypt (about 1250 B.C.). The law was delivered to the people by Moses, who claimed that it was of divine origin. Part of this law includes the Ten Commandments (Exodus, 20: 3-17), but Hebrew law included much more than this. The Pentateuch, the first five books of the Old Testament, contains numerous references to law. Especially in Exodus and Deuteronomy, we find detailed restrictions on diet, clothing, travel, warmaking, enslavement, and a good deal more. The law also stipulated appropriate types and degrees of punishments. In Exodus 21: 22, for example, we find the *lex talionis* described earlier: "You shall give life for life, tooth for tooth, hand for hand, foot for foot, burn for burn, wound for wound, stripe for stripe."

In the area of criminal law, the Hebrews made a very significant contribution to the advancement of modern legal principles. For example, the concept of individual moral responsibility has been attributed to Hebraic law (Kinnane, 1952: 179). Under most ancient legal systems, the clan or kin group was held accountable for the conduct of any of its members. There often was no notion of individual responsibility. Frequently, for example, if someone killed a member of another group, the victim's kin would retaliate against or demand reparation from the offending kin group. Blood feuds were common. They were seen as a means of restoring the honor of the injured group. When reparation was possible, it might involve the giving of livestock or some other form of compensation. Sometimes one of the offender's kin had to join the group of the victim to compensate for the loss. Hittite law, for example, provided that a slayer give four men or women to the family of the one slain (Schwartz, 1976: 37).

This concept of group accountability was replaced in Hebrew law by the idea of individual responsibility. The idea of vicarious liability (i.e., holding a person who is without fault liable for the transgression of another) was outlawed. Deuteronomy 24: 16, for example, provides that "The fathers shall not be put to death for the children; nor shall the children be put to death for the fathers; every man shall be put to death for his own sin." This prohibition is repeated in Numbers 35: 31, in which it is stated that "You shall accept no ransom for the life of a murderer, who is guilty of death; but he shall be put to death." This idea of individual responsibility was later carried over into Christianity, which influenced principles of law in most of the western world (Kinnane, 1952: 179-180).

Roman Law

Our discussion of early systems of law would not be complete without some reference to Roman law. The record of Roman law begins about

450 B.C. with the Twelve Tables, which are said to have formalized then existing customs. This early code is reminiscent of Babylonian and Mosaic law in that it included the *lex talionis*. Unlike most other early legal codes, however, the Roman law was thoroughly secular.

Early Roman law was given to procedural formalities and ceremonies. Although the early procedures were cumbersome and ritualistic, during subsequent centuries the Romans showed a talent for legal administration that was to become an important part of their legacy. They also demonstrated an unprecedented concern for the protection of individual rights against arbitrary governmental power. Rome established a republican form of government that included some popular representation, separation of powers, and a system of checks and balances.

Throughout much of its development the Roman legal system had two bodies of law. The *jus civile* was reserved for Roman citizens and consisted largely of ancient customs. However, after Rome extended her power over much of the known world—thereby incorporating foreigners who previously had not been subject to Roman law—a new body of law, *jus gentium,* was created. Because the foreigners were from many different states that had many different legal systems, judges had to search for legal principles that would be applicable to all. In this search the Roman magistrates were influenced profoundly by the Greeks, who had attempted to incorporate abstract principles of ethics and morality into their law. Following the Greek example, the Romans grounded the new law in a theory of "natural law" (that is, in an appeal to eternal and unalterable principles of right and justice). Eventually, *jus gentium* was made applicable to both Romans and non-Romans.

Perhaps the best known expression of the Roman idea of natural law is found in the writings of Cicero. In *The Republic,* he wrote: "True law is right reason in agreement with nature. It is of universal application, unchanging and everlasting." The notion that law can be made to reflect unassailable universal principles of right and justice is an important, and also a controversial, legacy of Roman law. For example, during the formative stages in the development of both English common law and American law after independence from England, judges routinely justified their decisions through appeals to natural law. It was not until the nineteenth century that the notion of natural law was to be challenged seriously by those who alleged that enacted law is largely a reflection of culturally bounded customs and an expression of power that bears little or no relationship to universal truth.

In the first few centuries A.D., Roman law became highly developed.

In terms of the scope of matters governed by law, the principles of justice embodied in law, and legal administration, Roman law was sophisticated and elaborate. It was to become a model for developing legal systems throughout western Europe. Although Rome fell in 476 A.D., its legal system was not lost. A major development took place in the sixth century, when the emperor Justinian commanded that the Roman law be codified. Much of the Justinian Code eventually was adopted by the Roman Catholic Church, whose canon law is grounded firmly in secular Roman principles. Later, much of Roman law was absorbed into the developing secular law on the European continent and, to a lesser extent, in England.

THE HISTORY AND DEVELOPMENT
OF ENGLISH COMMON LAW

We turn now to England, whose legal system was to have a profound effect on our own. English common law developed over seven centuries prior to the American Revolution. Although the origin of common law is generally placed at 1066, the year of the Norman Conquest, to understand its beginnings we must look back to the primitive laws and customs of the Germanic tribes that settled in various parts of England in ancient times.

Anglo-Saxon Roots of English Common Law

The roots of common law can be traced to the Anglo-Saxon period (5th-11th centuries), a time before England became a unified nation. We do not know a great deal about Anglo-Saxon law. Little of it was reduced to writing. Occasionally kings or tribal chiefs issued "dooms" (commands) which set forth some of the customary law in written form, but these decrees were probably not complete statements of the law (Pollock and Maitland, 1895: 27). The law was passed on largely by word of mouth and consisted of ancient and sacred customs enforced by tribal courts or councils. Many of these customary laws originally belonged to nomadic tribes whose law was tied to a group of people and not to a territory. As agriculture developed and as various tribes settled more permanently into certain regions, however, law was transformed from the rules that governed a tribe as it moved from place to place to standards that governed all the residents of a particular locality.

During the early Anglo-Saxon period, social organization was built around bonds of kinship. Conflicts between kin groups often erupted into blood feuds. The family that was wronged had the customary right and obligation to avenge one of their number. The family of the offending party had the duty either to make amends for the misdeed or to do battle. The aim of the new law that emerged during this early period was apparently limited to preserving the peace by developing means other than blood feuds for satisfying the desire for revenge (Pollock and Maitland, 1895: 31; Pound, 1939: 24).

The dooms of King Ethelbert, written in the sixth century, are the first records historians possess of Anglo-Saxon law. They suggest that law was concerned almost exclusively with acts of violence. In a brief statement consisting of 90 clauses, Ethelbert specified the manner of dealing with a variety of injuries to life and limb (for instance, from manslaughter to such offenses as breaking a man's thigh and pulling his hair). Only a few clauses dealt with property offenses. These were confined to housebreaking and cattle stealing (Simpson, 1981: 6-7). There was no mention at all to matters of contract, real estate, commerce, or any of the other topics that make up the bulk of modern law. Such issues were largely irrelevant to these simple agricultural peoples.

A peculiarity of Anglo-Saxon law and of most other early legal systems is that it made no distinction between injuries that were intentional and those that were accidental. Liability was based on the mere causation of harm. For example, Ploscowe cites an old English compilation of laws holding that:

> If someone in the sport of archery or other form of exercise kill another with a missile or by some such accident, let him repay, for the law is that he who commits evil unknowingly must pay for it knowingly [1939: 78].

This principle of absolute liability held persons responsible not only for accidental harms caused by them, but also for harms done by their slaves (who were viewed as property), animals, and even inanimate objects. For example, if a man's sword, in the hands of a third party, was the cause of death of another man, the sword's owner was held liable for the death (Pollock and Maitland, 1895: 472). Absolute liability was to remain a feature of English law long after the Norman Conquest. Neither lack of intent to do harm nor self-defense were accepted as bases of exemption from criminal liability until well into the thirteenth century. It was at that point in history that medieval scholars began to study Roman law and to consider distinctions based on the intent of the offender.

Each offense in Anglo-Saxon times carried an accompanying sanction, which usually took the form of a money payment called *bot* to atone or compensate for the injury.

Bot . . . was set at a certain number of shillings in case of wounding; a
higher number if the wound injured not only the flesh but also the bone;
indemnity had to be higher if the bone was broken. And so it went with
other injuries. An injury to the ear had to be compensated by a certain
amount, and the amount was greater if the hearing as well as the ear were
affected. If teeth were struck out the penalty for the front teeth was greater
than for those on the side which supposedly were less important. Some
fingers were valued at more than others due to the kinds of weapons in
use, and the price was scaled accordingly [Kinnane, 1952: 215].

If a person was killed by another, *bot* was set at the *wergild*, the value of
the deceased's life. Like some other archaic legal systems, Anglo-Saxon
law took account of the rank of the injured party in determining
appropriate compensation. For example, the *wergild* for nobility was
six times that of the common man. The *wergild* was even higher for the
king and was higher still for high-ranking clergy. What is perhaps most
important to recognize is that it was possible to atone for every harm,
including murder, by paying money to the victim's kin. This clearly
suggests that our modern conception of crime was largely unknown to
these people. All injuries seem to have been viewed as private,
amendable wrongs (Seagle, 1941: 29).

Payment of *bot* to the injured's kin was apparently an unsatisfactory
method of averting the blood feud. Feuds continued, and they may even
have been approved by law (Pollock and Maitland, 1911: 451). There
was no state as we know it. There were no law enforcement professionals. Consequently, there was no mechanism for enforcing payment
of the *bot*.

During the later Anglo-Saxon period, when feudalism had become
more firmly established, a new form of payment, the *wite*, was created. It
involved a fine paid directly to either a local lord or the king. What is
perhaps most significant about *wite*, aside from its obvious exploitation
of offenses to build revenues, is that it is the first indication we have that
some law violations were treated as something other than personal or
private matters. The *wite* symbolizes the notion that some offenses are
more than harms to individuals for which the offender can atone. They
also are injurious to the public welfare that the sovereign is charged with
protecting. Further, whereas *bot* involved compensation or reparation,
wite seems clearly to have involved a form of punishment. That the state
has a direct interest in crime and that crimes are deserving of
punishment were to become central ideas in the development of modern
criminal jurisprudence.

The idea of law and of legal development during the Anglo-Saxon
period is of considerable historical as well as contemporary interest.

According to the thinking of the time, law was not supposed to be "made" by anyone. It was instead "found" in ancient customs that were "the possession of the people, preserved in the memory of men [and] declared by them in their local assemblies" (Cam, 1963: 12). Custom had an almost sacred quality to it:

> Literally all law was felt to be eternally valid and in some degree sacred, as the providence of God was conceived to be a universally present force which touched men's lives even in their most trifling details. The custom which was rooted in the folkways was in no sense cut off from natural law but rather was felt to be a twig of the great tree of the law, which grew from earth to heaven and in whose shade all human life was lived [Sabine and Thorson, 1973: 196].

Custom governed all matters that needed to be adjudicated. When new circumstances arose, the thought was not that new law needed to be created but that the established customs needed to be examined to understand what they truly meant and to apply them to the new situation. This method of building new law was to become an important feature of the evolution both of English common law and of law in the United States.

In the later Anglo-Saxon period, kin-based councils gave way to more politically administered justice. A number of different courts were created. On the highest level were county courts made up of noblemen and presided over by bishops. (At that time, there was no distinction between ecclesiastical and secular law.) The county courts were supplemented by "hundred" courts—assemblies of freemen who met monthly to handle disputes in a smaller geographical area—and by "hall moots"—private courts presided over by lords who had jurisdiction over matters involving their tenants. Once the *wite* had become firmly established as a customary method of dispute resolution, there was substantial revenue to be derived from holding court. Thus, citizens were increasingly pressed to bring their disputes before these administrative bodies.

Court procedures differed dramatically from those we use today. There were no prosecutors. The offended party had to initiate the action personally. Furthermore, there was nothing even roughly resembling the modern version of a trial. Guilt or innocence were determined through trial by oath and trial by ordeal. Trial by oath required the accused to make a formal statement declaring his innocence before God and his countrymen. The idea seems to have been that God would intervene to cause the guilty to falter before the oath was completed.

Interestingly, this method of proof was available only to free men of good reputation who had no criminal record (Hyams, 1981: 93). It was not available to slaves and serfs, who were forced to undergo the ordeal. Trial by ordeal was far more common. It required that the accused perform some physical test whose outcome was taken as a sign from God of the accused's guilt or innocence. For example, one ordeal required that the accused carry a red-hot iron in his palm for a distance of nine feet. The hand was then wrapped. If in three days the wound was clean, the accused was considered to be innocent. If the wound festered, he was judged to be guilty. This manner of proof, which almost always resulted in a finding of guilt, continued well into the thirteenth century.

The Development of Common Law

After the Norman Conquest of 1066, William the Conqueror and his successors introduced major social and legal changes by claiming ownership of all the land in England and by using the authority of the king as ruler of the entire land to centralize and unify the court system. They appointed their own representatives to the local councils, replaced the local nobility, and separated the secular and ecclesiastical courts so that state law became distinct from canon law. The early British kings also extended the notion of the *king's peace*, an idea that had existed in only rudimentary form under the weaker Anglo-Saxon rulers. King's peace involved the idea that certain persons, places, and time periods were under the protection of the king. If this protection was violated by violence or feuding, it was taken as an affront to the king. In this way, the king obtained jurisdiction over many wrongs that previously had been heard in the local courts (Pound, 1939: 26). Over time, the jurisdiction of the king's peace was expanded in such a manner that the royal courts had jurisdiction over almost all legal matters.

During the reign of Henry II (1154-1189), a system of centralized royal courts was initiated, and a complex system was used to obtain relief from the courts. When someone applied to the king for justice, he issued a letter to the local authorities (a "writ") directing what action should be taken. These writs had to be purchased, and they became an important source of revenue for the crown. The writ system was complex. There was a separate writ for every form of relief that could be sought. The creation of the royal courts and the complexity of the writs led to the development of the legal profession. Judges who were trained in the law began to preside in the court system. Some presided over the central courts, whereas others ("judges in eyre") made periodic circuits of the countryside. These itinerant judges merged the diverse regional customs into a common law that was uniformly interpreted throughout England.

By the thirteenth century, a central, independent court, the King's Bench, was established to hear criminal cases. It was supplemented on the local level by regional criminal courts. Through these courts, uniform definitions were supplied for a range of customary crimes (for example, murder, manslaughter, rape, robbery, burglary, arson, sodomy, mayhem, and numerous other lesser offenses), a range of punishments associated with each offense was developed, and new procedures were established for bringing persons to answer to criminal charges and for adjudicating guilt or innocence. Some of the more important changes that took place are described below.

First and perhaps most importantly, the notion of crime was transformed from an injury to an individual or a kin group to an injury to the state. The state's role in criminal matters shifted from that of a neutral party overseeing the resolution of a private dispute to that of the initiator of a criminal prosecution. Punishments (usually fines and forfeiture of lands) were ordered on behalf of the crown, and the earlier concern with compensation of the victim diminished. The old system of blood feud and of *bot* and *wergild* gradually died out.

Second, trial by ordeal was supplemented in the king's courts by trial by combat (jousting, duels) and eventually trial by jury as the chief method of ascertaining the truth in criminal cases. Initiated in the thirteenth century, jury trials were not as we know them today, although they were a step toward rationality compared to the earlier mystical forms of proof. The accused was brought before a group of his countrymen who rendered a verdict based on what they knew of the defendant rather than from evidence presented to them (Pound, 1939: 66). Often the trial outcome was predetermined by the mere selection of jurors. Still, jury trials represented a significant improvement over trial by ordeal, as the latter method almost invariably resulted in a finding of guilt. Later, during the sixteenth and seventeenth centuries, significant advances were made in the method of jury trial. Steps were taken to insure that juries were comprised of impartial individuals, and jurors were charged with reaching a verdict based solely on testimony and evidence presented at the trial.

Third, between the thirteenth and the eighteenth centuries, the adversary system was born. An elaborate system of procedural safeguards was developed to protect the rights of the accused. The adversary system is thought to have originated with trial by combat. The idea evolved that truth was best served by having opposing parties contend against each other. In this system, opposing counsel examine and cross-examine witnesses and take the initiative in presenting evidence to persuade the judge or the jury that its side should prevail. Judges in such a system are independent referees between the battling parties. They assure that the parties fight fairly.[1] The requirements of procedural fairness eventually came to include the right to a jury trial, the right to representation by counsel, the right to confront witnesses, and the defendant's privilege against compelled self-incrimination. These and other protections for the accused were part of the common law by the seventeenth century, and most were subsequently incorporated into the American Bill of Rights.

Fourth, over the centuries England was transformed from a largely rural, agricultural society into an urban, industrialized nation. The law developed accordingly and came to govern a wide range of matters for which there had earlier been little need. The criminal law was greatly expanded to include a multitude of minor offenses dealing with matters of public order (for example, prohibitions against drunkenness, disorderly conduct, and vagrancy), numerous property offenses that earlier had been treated as essentially private matters (for instance, various forms of larceny and embezzlement), and offense involving personal injury that traditionally had not been part of criminal law.

The English Method of Law Making

Frequently, common law is described as "customary law." However, this does not mean that the common law enforced customary modes of conduct. If that had been the case, the law would have been inflexible and thoroughly wedded to rules established during Anglo-Saxon times. We already have seen that the common law developed considerably beyond its Anglo-Saxon beginnings, and now we will explore how this came about.

During the Anglo-Saxon period, law was largely synonymous with custom. However, customary law took on new meaning following the Norman Conquest. It was virtually impossible for the royal courts to reconcile the diverse customs of the various regions of England that had been brought under centralized control. Consequently, the courts had to select from among existing customs those that would be given the force of law and to establish new "customs" to govern matters about which existing customs were silent. As Pound (1939: 56) has observed: "The king's courts conceived of themselves as administering the custom or the common law of England. But there was in fact no such general body of custom common to all England." It is important to note that judges spoke as if there were such a general custom. This gave the appearance of legitimacy to their decisions. There was a general "belief that judicial decision was ascertaining and declaring the established custom of the land" (Pound, 1939: 57).

Common law, in other words, was largely judge-made law. In the area of criminal law, for example, it was left to the courts to define what acts constituted crimes, what defenses and excuses might exempt a defendant from criminal liability, and what punishments attached to criminal offenses. That common law originated in the courts can perhaps be explained in terms of two factors. First, the tradition of judge-made law already had been firmly established in the Anglo-Saxon period. The Norman kings made no attempt to change this custom. Second, judges were accorded very high prestige because, being formally trained in the law, they gave the appearance of being intimately familiar with customary practices. It is not surprising, then, that law was seen as the proper province of the courts rather than of kings or criminal offenses.

Common law is customary law, then, in the sense that it traditionally emerged from the courts. It is also customary in the sense that a unique method of deciding cases was devised by common law judges. Specifically, English courts developed the doctrine of *stare decisis* ("let the decision stand"). This required that new cases be decided in a fashion consistent with principles of law established in the resolution of prior cases (precedents). Precedents were deemed to be binding sources of authority whose application to subsequent cases would produce "correct" results. In practice this meant that when a court was presented with a case that was substantially similar to one that had been decided previously, the judge theoretically was bound to decide the matter in the same way that it was decided earlier. When asked to render a decision in a case that involved a somewhat novel set of issues or circumstances, the court would reason by analogy with principles established in prior cases to reach the "correct" result. Through this very conservative method, the common law gradually evolved. It elaborated and modified previously defined principles as new circumstances required.

The method of *stare decisis* began early in the history of common law but did not become fully established until the eighteenth century. Before the method could become a customary feature of judicial decision making, there had to be some means of recording prior decisions.

Initially law was not written. It existed only in the minds and oral pronouncements of judges. Written reporting of cases began in 1225, when Henry de Bracton reported 2,000 cases decided during the reign of Henry III. Bracton recorded the judgments that had been rendered and commented on the legal principles involved in each case. These manuscripts provided a guide for later courts that wished to look to past decisions for the principles to be applied in new cases. After Bracton's death, reporting continued through the *Year Books* (1268-1535), Sir Edward Coke's *Reports* (1572-1616), Matthew Hale's *Pleas of the Crown* (1682), and, perhaps most influential of all, Blackstone's *Commentaries on the Laws of England* (1765-1769). Blackstone's work is generally regarded as the most authoritative guide to principles of English common law. It was widely read and distributed in the United States at the time of the American Revolution and contributed significantly to the development of law in this country.

Several points need to be made about judge-made law in general and about use of the doctrine of *state decisis* in particular. First, it should be recognized that through the doctrine of *stare decisis* "judges and jurists strenuously denied that courts had the right to make law . . . The judge was to find and apply the right norm, nothing more" (Friedman, 1975: 240). Law was conceived to be a science that involved study of past decisions, discovery of the underlying principles embodied in them, and the application of these principles to changing times and circumstances. Not unlike the courts in Anglo-Saxon times, judges at common law appeared to be "finding" rather than "making" the law. The doctrine of *stare decisis* thus served an important legitimizing function by suggesting that the courts' judgments were products of disinterested and objective applications of time-honored principles and not the personal preferences of judges. Today this notion is embodied in the frequently stated maxim that "Ours is a government of laws, not of men." In fact, however, some precedents were followed and some were not. Frequently, the meanings of past decisions were unclear and contrary precedents often existed that might support widely divergent outcomes of new cases. Thus, the appeal to precedent was—and still is—sometimes used quite efectively to mask the raw exercise of judicial power (Kairys, 1982).

Second, the reliance on courts rather than on legislative bodies to make law made it virtually inevitable that the common law would evolve in a piecemeal fashion. Some areas of the law became highly developed. Others remained rudimentary. Just how complex the law in any area became was an artifact of the number of cases in that area that the courts were asked to hear and agreed to decide. In other words, the law did not develop through a process of advance planning and deliberation. It arose through after-the-fact realizations that problems were created by adhering to existing principles that no longer produced desired results.

Third, throughout most of the history of common law there was no coherent statement of the law to be found anywhere. The law existed only in the reporting of thousands of judicial decisions over hundreds of years. If one were to develop a comprehensive understanding of the law in a given area, one had to pore through and study this mass of decisions.[2] Eventually, it became necessary that this unwieldy accumulation of decisions be distilled in statutory form.

The move to enact legislation in England began during the reign of Henry II. Another milestone occurred in 1215, when the Magna Carta was signed by King John. In the sixteenth century, Parliament began preparing and enacting legislation. However, because all of this legislation was subject to interpretation and review by the courts, the common law continued to grow. The courts regularly reviewed legislation to give precise meaning to its wording, to make the intent of statutes clear, and to determine their applicability to a variety of situations. It also was the duty of the courts to consider whether statutory law was consistent with customary principles (the "law of the land") and to negate legislation when it ran afoul of these principles. Statutes played a relatively insignificant role in English law until the nineteenth century.

THE DEVELOPMENT OF AMERICAN LAW

When the first settlers came to the colonies, they were afforded the rights and privileges of English citizens and were subject to English law. However, they had little need for an elaborate system of law. The population was small and largely homogeneous. The economy was fairly simple. Many of the complex rules and regulations that governed all facets of British life seemed unnecessary. Further, for a long time there were no lawyers and few law books. Still, the customary law of England was preserved in a somewhat simplified form in the colonies.

Beginning in 1675, English supervision of Colonial America began in earnest with the establishment of the Privy Council, which reviewed colonial legislation to insure that it was in accord with the common law. In addition to supervision by the Privy Council, other forces worked to insure that law in the colonies adhered closely to common law principles and procedures. Many law students studied in the English Inns of Court, where they lived together and received training in the traditions of the common law under the tutelage of judges (Kempin, 1973). Upon their return to the colonies, they served as preceptors (tutors) to other law students. Also, it is estimated that 2500 copies of Blackstone's *Commentaries* were sold in Colonial America. This work apparently had great influence and helped to promote the preservation of common law both prior to and following American independence.

Immediately following independence, the common law of crimes was accepted and followed in the former colonies to a remarkable degree. Frequently this was accomplished by adopting the common law or parts thereof through express legislative enactment. In other states the common law was adopted through a decision of the courts:

> The English common law, so far as it is reasonable in itself, suitable to the conditions of our people, and consistent with the letter and spirit of our federal and state constitutions and statutes, has been and is followed by our courts, and may be said to consititute part of the common law of Ohio [*Bloom v. Richards*, 2 Ohio 387, 390 (1853)].

In still other states, the common law was incorporated through constitutional provisions. The original Constitution of New York (1777), for example, states,

> And this convention doth further, in the name and by the authority of the good people of this state, ordain, determine, and declare that such parts of the common law of England, and of the statute law of England and Great Britain, and of the acts of the legislature of the colony of New York, as together did form the law of the said colony in the year of our Lord one thousand seven hundred and seventy-five, shall be and continue the law of this state, subject to such alterations and provisions as the legislature of this state shall, from time to time, make concerning the same.

Most states that accepted the common law of crimes adopted both its substantive criminal law and its law of criminal procedure. *Substantive criminal law* defines what conduct is criminal, specifies what the state must prove with respect to each offense, prescribes the punishments associated with each offense, and defines defenses and excuses to criminal liability. The *law of criminal procedure* regulates the steps in the processing of criminal cases, defining both the rights of the accused (for example, right to counsel, right to speedy trial) and limits on governmental power (for instance, restrictions on police powers of arrest and search).

At the time of American independence, the common law of crimes consisted of thousands of cases dealing with matters of both substantive and procedural criminal law. The sentiment soon developed that crimes needed to be stated in a form that would give citizens clear notice of what conduct was both forbidden and required. Consequently, beginning in the eighteenth century, federal and state legislatures departed from the common law tradition of judge-made law by enacting statutes. Most of them specifically recognized many common law crimes and simply restated them in statutory form. In other instances common law definitions of criminal offenses were modified by expanding the scope of the conduct included in the offense or, more often, by redefining the punishment to make it less severe. The legislatures also created hundreds of new offenses unknown at common law.

During the nineteenth century, the body of substantive criminal law had become truly massive. Many offenses were ancient and clearly irrelevant to modern life. Consequently, many states undertook major reforms by creating systematic, revised compilations of statutory offenses. In about half the states, common law crimes were expressly or implicitly abolished. In the other half, state codes managed to retain common law crimes through "reception statutes." In Florida, for example, the penal code provides that "the common law of England in relation to crimes, except so far as the same relates to the modes and degrees of punishment, shall be of full force in this state where there is no existing provision by statute on the subject" (Florida Statutes Annotated, Section 775.01).

In those states that abolished the common law of crimes and in the federal jurisdiction, which long ago rejected the idea that federal courts have the authority to punish acts that are not defined as crimes by Congress, the common law still retains considerable importance. In all states and in the federal jurisdiction one can find instances of statutory offenses that were offenses at common law. One can also find terms and concepts that were used at common law in the statutory descriptions of crimes as well as in the delineation of defenses and excuses to criminal liability. In such instances it may be necessary to go back to the common law to define these terms and to give them proper interpretation. Courts in both the states and the federal jurisdiction currently use common law principles in the interpretation of statutory and constitutional provisions. The abiding significance of the common law is well summarized in the following excerpt from a Massachusetts case:

To a very great extent, the unwritten law [common law] constitutes the basis of our jurisprudence, and furnishes the rules by which public and private rights are established and secured, the social relations of all persons regulated, their rights, duties, and obligations determined, and all violations of duty redressed and punished. Without its aid, the written law, embracing the Constitution and statute laws, would constitute but a lame, partial, and impracticable system. Even in many cases where statutes have been made in respect to particular subjects, they could not be carried into effect, and must remain a dead letter, without the aid of the common law. In cases of murder and manslaughter, the statute declares the punishment; but what acts shall constitute murder, what manslaughter, or what justifiable or excusable homicide, are left to be decided by the rules and principles of the common law . . . Indeed . . . without the common law, our legislation and jurisprudence would be impotent, and wholly deficient in completeness and symmetry [*Commonwealth v. Chapman*, 54 Mass. 68, 69 (1849)].

CURRENT SOURCES OF AMERICAN CRIMINAL LAW

Although common law continues to have a pervasive influence, contemporary criminal law emanates from several other sources. Each shapes the content and character of our legal system. Four sources of law dominate the contemporary scene: constitutions (the United States Constitution and the constitutions of each of the 50 states), legislated (statutory) law, judge-made (case) law, and administrative law. Each of these is briefly discussed below.

Constitutions as Sources of Criminal Law

The federal Constitution sets forth the distribution of powers among the executive, judicial, and legislative branches of government, specifies the scope of the powers of each branch, and outlines in general terms the basic rights and duties of American citizens. The federal Constitution represents the highest form of law in this country. No other form of law may conflict with it.

Although the provisions of the federal Constitution—most especially those contained in the Bill of Rights—have played an exceedingly influential role in shaping the development of the law of criminal procedure, only a few sections relate directly to substantive criminal law. For example, the Constitution creates some federal crimes directly (for instance, treason) and delegates to Congress the power to enact criminal legislation with respect to the specific matters over which Congress is given authority (for example, laws relating to taxation and interstate commerce). However, the bulk of the responsibility for developing the substantive law of crimes is retained by the states.

The relatively few directly relevant constitutional provisions regarding substantive criminal law notwithstanding, it must be understood that the Constitution is a significant document for those concerned with this area of law. Perhaps most important, constitutional provisions are almost never self-explanatory or self-executing. They must be interpreted, and in our system of government that interpretation is a responsibility of the judicial branch. The manner in which the judiciary has constructed interpretations of the language of the Constitution has played a critical role in shaping the body of criminal law to which all of us are subject.

Statutes as Sources of Criminal Law

Most substantive criminal law today consists of statutory law (i.e., laws enacted by the United States Congress, the legislatures of each of the 50 states, and by the elected representatives of municipal governments). In a decided break with the English tradition of judge-made law, this nation set out on a course of formulating crimes through legislative enactment shortly after independence from British rule. As conceived in the Constitution, the function of law making belonged to legislative bodies rather than to courts, whose role, at least in theory, was restricted to legal interpretation and adjudication.

At least two important differences between statutory law and judge-made law should be noted. First, judge-made law is inherently conservative. Because it is built on precedents, it is tied to the past and does not readily adapt to social, political, and economic change. Legislators have greater freedom to make major innovations—although, of course, this freedom does not prevent them from being conservative or unwilling to change. Second, legislators, being elected representatives, are more responsive than judges to public pressures to create new law and to make alterations in existing law. The history of criminal law in this country can be seen largely as a response to pressures exerted upon legislators by specialized interest groups to devise new methods of controlling persons and conditions perceived as troublesome.

During the nineteenth and early twentieth centuries, the state and federal legislatures enacted a multitude of statutory provisions defining criminal offenses. Aside from extensions and modifications of the common law discussed earlier, whole areas of behavior that were previously unregulated were criminalized. Criminal laws were enacted to regulate railroads, banking, transportation, communication, the manufacture, distribution, and sale of consumer goods, and a host of other business activities. Many "victimless" crimes were created (for instance, prohibitions against gambling, possession of obscene literature, alcohol use, and the use of opiates and other narcotic substances). Beyond these offenses, there was a massive proliferation of statutory law creating an ill-conceived assortment of crimes of a relatively trivial or marginal nature. The Florida Criminal Code, for example, contains prohibitions against tattooing (Section 877.04) and artificially coloring chickens and rabbits (Section 828.161). As the sociologist Robert Park 1978: (10-11) has observed, "We are always passing laws in America. We might as well get up and dance. The laws are largely to relieve emotion, and the legislatures are quite aware of that fact."

Judicial Decisions (Case Law)
as Sources of Criminal Law

The law making function exercised by common law judges was largely abolished in the United States. Nevertheless, courts clearly do make law. Perhaps the most well-known illustrations of this law making function lie outside the area of criminal law. In the case of *Brown v. Board of Education of Topeka* (347 U.S. 483 [1954]), for example, the United States Supreme Court established a precedent with sweeping implications when it forbade segregation in the nation's public schools on the grounds that it violated the equal protection clause of the Fourteenth Amendment of the Constitution. Clearly, the court's decision was an act of legislation as well as interpretation. Though perhaps less well known, the courts have also shaped the development of criminal law in multiple and significant ways through constitutional and statutory interpretation.

Law Making Through
Constitutional Interpretation

The Supreme Court's role as the ultimate authority on matters of Constitutional law was first enunciated in the celebrated case of *Marbury v. Madison* (5 U.S. 137 [1803]). By virtue of the high court's power to review, interpret, and invalidate state and federal laws, state constitutional provisions, and lower federal and state court decisions when they are alleged to conflict with provisions of the United States Constitution, the Supreme Court is an extremely powerful force in the shaping of American law.

It is as a result of its interpretation by the Supreme Court over the years that the Constitution has become a significant source of procedural protections for the criminally accused. Many of the procedural protections found in our Bill of Rights—including right to counsel, protection against unreasonable searches and seizures, right to trial by jury, and many more—were provided at common law to one degree or another. However, although common law may have provided the basis both for their acceptance in principle as rights accruing to American citizens and for initial interpretations as to their substance and scope, they have been significantly modified and expanded over time through an ongoing process of judicial review.

In the area of substantive criminal law, the Supreme Court has been active as well. On numerous occasions, it has struck down state criminal laws found to violate the Constitution. For example, in the highly controversial decision of *Roe v. Wade* (410 U.S. 113 [1972]), the Court struck down a Texas statute that made it a crime for a woman to obtain an abortion on the grounds that the statute ran afoul of a constitutionally protected right to privacy. Similarly, in *Robinson v. California* (370 U.S. 660 [1962]), the Court ruled that a California statute criminalizing narcotic addiction was in violation of the Eighth Amendment's cruel and unusual punishments clause.

Law Making Through Statutory Interpretation

The judicial contribution to the law of crimes is not limited to interpretations of state and federal constitutions. Both federal and state courts also regularly interpret and apply statutory law. Very often criminal statutes are poorly drafted. Their language is ambiguous or obsolete. Suppose, for example that a state passes legislation that defines the carrying of a concealed weapon as an unlawful act. But what does the word "concealed" mean? And precisely what types of objects warrant being defined as weapons? The true meaning of such terms is often not explicitly stated in criminal statutes. Thus, these are typical areas for judicial interpretation.

In interpreting the meaning of a statute that is ambiguous the courts generally will try to determine the legislature's intent, but there are no clear and precise rules for doing so. As Justice Holmes has observed: "every question of [statutory] construction is unique, and an argument that would prevail in one case may be inadequate in another" (*United States v. Jin Fuey Moy*, 242 U.S. 394, 402 [1916]). Thus, the Court often cannot avoid making law by construing a statute in a particular way: "When a judge tries to find out what government would have intended which it did not say, he puts into its mouth things it ought to have said, and that is very close to substituting what he himself thinks is right" (Hand, cited in Mermin, 1982: 257).

Administrative Regulations as Sources of Criminal Law

The fourth and final source of law in this country consists of rules developed by administrative agencies. There are hundreds of such agencies (for instance, the Food and Drug Administration, the Environmental Protection Agency, and the Internal Revenue Service). They exist on both the federal and state level. They are created by legislative bodies in an effort to regulate such concerns as business, health, welfare, agriculture, professions, resource utilization, labor, and many other concerns that the legislature has neither the time nor the expertise to regulate and supervise independently.

The volume of law produced by these regulatory agencies greatly exceeds that of all federal and state statutory law. Moreover, the breadth of administrative law is sweeping. Administrative agencies provide standards for such things as the air we breathe and the water that we drink, the foodstuffs and drugs that we purchase, housing and construction, education, worker safety, licensing of occupations and businesses, and much more.

Depending on its statutory authority, each administrative agency has the power to issue rules and regulations and to deal with rule violations. Responses to administrative rule violations take a number of noncriminal forms (for example, suspension or revocation of licenses, cease-and-desist orders, recall of products, denial of benefits, and monetary penalties). In addition, however, legislative bodies often delegate to administrative agencies the power to create regulations whose violation constitutes a crime. This practice was first approved in the case of *United States v. Grimaud* (220 U.S. 506 [1911]), which involved a challenge to the Secretary of Agriculture's power to create regulations that carried criminal penalties. (The defendant in the case had grazed his sheep on government land without first obtaining a permit required by a regulation of the Department of Agriculture.) The Supreme Court ruled that there is no constitutional violation so long as Congress establishes the criminal penalties attached to administrative regulations.

Since the *Grimaud* decision, numerous challenges to the creation and enforcement of administrative crimes have been heard by the courts. These challenges have established the following limits on administrative crimes: (1) the determination of which regulations shall carry criminal penalties must be made by the legislature and not by the administrative agency; (2) the legislature must set forth standards to guide administrative agencies in determining which kinds of regulations will carry criminal penalties; (3) and the trial of persons charged with administrative crimes must take place in criminal courts, not merely in tribunals established by administrative agencies.

SUMMARY

The purpose of this chapter has been to provide an overview of the basic nature of law, to develop an appreciation for the history of our legal system, and to examine contemporary sources of law in this country. We have seen that systems of law have been an important part of social life for at least 4,000 years and that, even in ancient times, some civilizations possessed highly detailed legal codes. Many of the concepts embodied in these ancient systems of law survive to the present day.

We also have seen that our legal system is by no means an American invention. Our system of law was developing for several hundred years on English soil. That history begins with the Anglo-Saxon period, when social and economic conditions required only a rather crude system of law. Kin-based tribal groups settled disputes through feuds and compensation. What law there was seems to have been directed almost entirely toward atoning for acts of violence.

A radical and abrupt change took place following the Norman Conquest of 1066. England became a unified nation with a centralized court system. The royal courts amalgamated the regional customs that had existed prior to unification into a "common law" for the new nation. Although originally rooted in Anglo-Saxon custom, common law was subsequently influenced by canon law, Roman law, and by judicial interpretation of precedents. In the area of criminal law, this meant that judges defined crimes and established the penalties attached to them. Many of our contemporary definitions of crimes (e.g., murder, manslaughter, robbery, arson, and rape) are derived directly from English common law. Common law evolved slowly through the judicial practice of relying on doctrinal principles established in precedents to decide new cases. These principles were gradually modified as new issues and circumstances arose that required adjustments in the existing law. The use of this method gave legitimacy to the law and often masked the extent to which law making was an exercise of power rather than a scientific enterprise.

We have seen that the common law of England was accepted in this country to a remarkable degree. Many of our states adopted both the substantive and procedural common law of crimes in whole or in part. Although most crimes today consist of offenses unknown at common law, common law principles are still essential to interpretation of both constitutional provisions and legislative enactments.

Finally, it was shown that the major source of criminal law in England was the judiciary, but that in this country law emanates from multiple sources: constitutions, legislative enactments, the judiciary, and administrative agencies. Constitutions outline the broad contours of our legal system and are an especially important source of the law of criminal procedure. Case law continues as an important source of both substantive and procedural law as the courts carry out their function of statutory and constitutional interpretation. However, most substantive criminal law today is statutory law. Over the past 100 years, there has been a marked tendency to utilize the criminal law as a method of responding to newly perceived problems. The result has been a tremendous expansion in both legislatively created offenses and in administrative regulations carrying criminal penalties.

DISCUSSION QUESTIONS

1. In this chapter we have seen that most ancient civilizations viewed their legal codes as either a divinely inspired set of rules or as a compilation of customs that had an almost sacred quality to them. How does the modern view of law differ, and to what might the change be attributed.

2. Consider some of the benefits and liabilities of judge-made law versus statutory law.

3. We have noted that the modern tendency is to criminalize many minor or even trivial forms of deviance. What benefit is derived from passing laws that are largely unenforceable and for which there is little public support?

NOTES

1. The adversary system stands in marked contrast to the inquisitorial system that developed throughout most of continental Europe. In the inquisitorial system, the judge conducts and directs the pretrial inquiry into the crime, and all parties—counsel, witnesses, defendant—are expected to cooperate with the court. The trial itself proceeds in stages, most of which are not open to public view. Before entering the courtroom to hear oral argument, judges often will have studied the files, which include legal briefs submitted by both sides, and already may have reached a decision. On their own initiative, civil law judges gather, hear, and evaluate evidence, and control and guide the search for truth. Their domination of the proceedings leaves little room for cross-examination, which is considered the most effective method of arriving at the truth in the adversarial system, and lessens the role of juries, which traditionally has been considered vital in criminal proceedings in common law countries.

2. This is in marked contrast to the civil law tradition, which, borrowing a lesson from the Romans, developed a detailed system of statutory or legislated law. Civil law countries tend to have comprehensive and fairly intelligible penal codes. When a controversy arises in a civil law system, the court is asked to locate the governing statutory provision and to interpret its meaning in light of the problem at hand. Civil law systems are not wedded to history. Past cases are not entirely ignored, but judges are in no way bound by prior decisions of the courts. By contrast, in a common law system, the principle of *stare decisis* and the deference to precedent that it embodies, is essential. Common law builds on judicial experience, not legislated rules. There may be no statutory law at all, as indeed there was not during much of the common law's development.

end of file at end of Chapter 1

2

THE NATURE OF
CRIMINAL LAW

Criminal law is part of an enormous body of legal rules governing relations among individuals, groups, and the state. In fact, criminal law amounts to only a small portion of the law that governs us in our day-to-day interactions, and criminal cases constitute only a small fraction of the legal issues that come before our courts. Law regulates myriad noncriminal matters: the buying and selling of property (real estate law), the enforcement of formal agreements (the law of contracts), marriage, divorce, and adoption (domestic relations or family law), the political organization of the state and powers of governmental officials (constitutional law), claims involving personal injury and property damage (tort law), resource conservation and protection (environmental law), care of the mentally retarded and mentally ill (mental health and civil commitment law), the levying and payment of taxes (tax law), the protection of children (juvenile law), and a host of other matters. Law is also an important means by which we seek to attain a variety of goals, and none of these goals is the exclusive province of criminal law. Thus, one of the initial tasks before us is to determine what criminal law is and how it differs from other forms of law.

We can begin by making a purely classificatory distinction. Criminal law is a subfield of public law rather than of private law. *Private law* refers to law that concerns matters between private persons (individuals or corporations) that do not directly involve the state. Take, for example, the matter of a contested divorce. The legislature enacts law defining divorce and the grounds upon which divorce may be obtained. The law also outlines procedures to be followed by spouses to ensure that marriages are dissolved in an efficient, fair, and orderly way. However, the government does not become involved directly on the side of one of the litigants. The state claims no direct interest in the outcome. In theory if often not in practice, it seeks to provide the neutral forum of the court to facilitate the resolution of the matter. Moreover, if the party initiating the action should change his or her mind and decide not to pursue it, the state does not pursue it independently.

In contrast, *public law* is law that relates directly to the state in its political or sovereign capacity. Public law embraces such matters as the structure of government, the powers and duties of public officials, and the duties and obligations that private citizens and corporate entities owe to governmental authority. Criminal law is part of public law. Crime is viewed as an offense not merely or even primarily against an individual victim. It is an offense against the state.

Recall that during the Anglo-Saxon period the courts did not look upon murder, rape, robbery, and similar injuries as offenses against the state. They were seen as private matters between offenders and victims. The state did not bring an action against the offender. Its courts acted only as mediators. However, in the twelfth century the law began to differentiate between matters involving conduct that threatened the peace and welfare of society and matters that implicated private interests. With regard to the latter, the state continued in its role as dispute mediator, taking no interest in the matter other than to ensure that the injured party was compensated adequately by the offender for the harm suffered. With regard to the former, the state became an active participant as the party bringing legal action against the accused.

Criminal law is public law, then, because the state asserts a direct interest in protecting the community from behavior it has defined as crime. Unlike private litigation, in which it is incumbent upon the injured party to take action against the offender, the victim often plays a relatively minor role in a criminal proceeding. The government may prosecute a criminal defendant quite without regard to whether that action and purpose coincides with the wishes of the victim.

This distinction between public and private law does not adequately delimit the boundaries of criminal law. There are many forms of public law other than criminal law. For example, in the commitment of a mentally ill individual to an institution, the government may be the *plaintiff* (the party initiating the proceeding). Such an action constitutes a matter of public law, but it is not a criminal matter. Similarly, the adjudication of a child as a juvenile delinquent is a matter of public law even though it does not involve a criminal proceeding. We must look beyond the involvement of government as a party to distinguish criminal law from other forms of law.

Another distinction frequently made is that between criminal and civil law. *Civil law* encompasses all noncriminal matters, whether they be matters of public law (as in commitment of the mentally ill) or matters of private law (as in a suit for damages in a personal injury case).

Thus, we can say that criminal law is not civil law, but this does not take us very far. We need to consider characteristic features of criminal law that distinguish it from civil law. This can be done by focusing our attention on two questions. First, what if anything is distinctive about the behavior that falls within the reach of the criminal law? Second, is there something distinctive about the methods that criminal law uses to respond to rule violations?

THE SUBJECT MATTER OF CRIMINAL LAW

At least in theory, criminal law deals with subject matter that is distinct from all other forms of law. A fair statement of the general principle is that criminal law is concerned with *voluntary and intentional conduct that causes public harm.* As we shall see, criminal law theory differs from criminal law practice in many respects. However, let us begin by examining more closely the elements of the general principle just stated.

A Matter of Public Harm

Almost since the inception of common law the designation of certain harms as public harms has been central to an understanding of the logic underlying the difference between criminal and civil law. In his *Commentaries on the Laws of England,* Blackstone (1778: 5) described the emergent distinction as follows:

> The distinction of public wrongs from private, of crimes and misde-
> meanors from civil injuries, seems principally to consist of this: that
> private wrongs, or civil injuries, are an infringement or privation of the
> civil rights which belong to individuals, considered merely as individuals;
> public wrongs, or crimes and misdemeanors, are a breach and violation of
> the public rights and duties due to the whole community, considered as a
> community, in its social aggregate capacity.

It should be recalled that during the formative period in the development of common law, few offenses were recognized as crimes. These consisted of murder, manslaughter, rape, robbery, sodomy, larceny, burglary, arson, and mayhem. All of these are offenses *mala in se,* as offenses that are "evil in themselves." They are recognized almost universally as morally wrong, and there is little doubt that they pose a serious threat to society. Thus, at the time that the distinction between crimes and civil offenses emerged, criminal law was limited to behavior that was clearly socially injurious. Consequently, there was considerable validity to the notion that criminal law differed from civil law with respect to the types of harm that each seeks to control.

Over the centuries, however, literally hundreds of new offenses were added to the penal codes. Many criminalized acts that posed no clear threat to the social order. These are offenses *mala prohibita,* offenses that are said to be wrong only because they are prohibited by law and not because public sentiment regards them as immoral and socially injurious. Examples include prohibitions against being drunk in public, selling alcoholic beverages on Sunday, driving without a valid operator's license, and loitering. These offenses do not necessarily have the force of morality behind them, and the harm they cause to society is often questionable. Indeed, their classification as crimes often blurs the distinction between crimes and civil injuries.

The *mala in se-mala prohibita* distinction has little meaning today. The modern approach is to distinguish between felonies and misdemeanors. The basis for this distinction is largely associated with the punishment attached to various criminal offenses. A *felony* is commonly defined as an offense punishable by death or by imprisonment for more than one year in a state or federal prison. A *misdemeanor* is most often defined as an offense punishable by incarceration, usually in a local institution, for a period up to one year. The difference between felonies and misdemeanors does not correspond to that between *mala in se* and *mala prohibita* offenses. Many misdemeanors are *mala in se* offenses. Similarly, many felonies are *mala prohibita* offenses.

Furthermore, the distinction between public harms as the focus of the criminal law and private injuries as the focus of the civil law becomes even weaker when we consider some of the matters that are handled routinely by civil courts. Surely society is harmed in some sense whenever there is a breach of contract, a violation of antitrust law, racial discrimination in employment, or any of scores of other injuries that are matters of civil litigation (Hart, 1958). The simple fact of the matter is that not all of the social harms recognized by law are within the reach of the criminal law, and not all of the behavior defined as criminal is clearly socially harmful. Nonetheless, in theory criminal law is reserved for social harms and civil law is reserved for private injuries. The distinction may be largely fictitious, but it serves as an operating principle that justifies much of what is done in the name of the criminal law.

A Matter of "Evil-Meaning" Actors

It was stated above that the criminal law is theoretically restricted to voluntary and intentional conduct. This limitation rests on the rather unique concern of the criminal law with fixing moral blame rather than merely attributing responsibility. In other words, criminal liability is said to attach only when a socially harmful act is committed by a morally culpable actor (i.e., one who acts with evil intent).

> The contention that an injury can amount to a crime only when inflicted by intention is no provincial or transient notion. It is as universal and persistent in mature systems of law as belief in freedom of the human will and a consequent ability and duty of the normal individual to choose between good and evil. A relation between some mental element and punishment for a harmful act is almost as instinctive as the child's familiar exculpatory "But I didn't mean to" . . . Crime [is] a compound concept, generally constituted only from concurrence of an evil-meaning mind with an evil-doing hand [*Morrisette v. United States*, 342 U.S. 246, 252 (1952)].

To understand this concern with evil-meaning actors, it is important to remember the close historical connection between the concepts of crime and sin. Following the Norman Conquest, voluntary and intentional harms were distinguished from accidental harms. Only the former were designated as crimes. This was due largely to the influence of the ecclesiastical courts, which were primarily concerned with sin. Importantly, the notion of sin presupposes both freedom of choice and intentionality of action. At least in theory, criminal liability rests on these same foundations. There is an assumption that individuals are free to choose between good and evil. If they choose evil either by acting with the specific purpose of producing harm or by consciously disregarding a substantial risk of harm, then they are held criminally liable. Conversely, if they lack the intent to do harm or if they could not reasonably have foreseen the harmful consequences of their actions, their behavior, though harmful, is not deemed criminal. Thus, blameworthiness and not merely responsibility is the prerequisite for criminal punishment.

It is in the notion of the evil or morally culpable actor that we find a rational basis for much of the differentiation between criminal and civil law. For example, this notion is critical to the distinction between criminal law and the law of juvenile delinquency. Both are matters of public law. Both involve conduct that is socially harmful. Both may result in severe deprivations of liberty. However, matters involving children who commit acts that would be crimes if committed by adults are almost always handled by civil rather than criminal courts (but see Thomas and Bilchik, 1985, for a discussion of prosecuting juveniles in adult criminal courts). The reason is that children are presumed to lack the maturity and foresight to act with the kind of intent that justifies criminal liability. Thus, although the state may be concerned about the dangers posed by children who commit acts that would otherwise be crimes, it generally does not intervene through the method of the criminal law.

Because the notions of crime and moral culpability are so closely intertwined, we commonly absolve from criminal liability those who are unable to control their actions, those who are incompetent to make conscious choices, and those who do harm accidentally. The same concern for the actor's competence and purpose that usually protects children from the reach of the criminal law also protects the insane, those who make honest mistakes of fact, those who act under duress, and those whose actions constitute involuntary physical responses. (Each of these bases of immunity from criminal liability will be discussed in subsequent chapters).

The emphasis on moral culpability that characterizes the criminal law is not nearly so pervasive in civil law. Civil law is concerned primarily with compensating injuries and thus holds people to a higher standard of liability than the criminal law. Juveniles and the insane, for example, may be held civilly liable for harms caused by their actions even though they may escape criminal liability.

The notion of immoral conduct is so critical to criminal law that sometimes the law is activated even when the intended harm did not occur—provided, of course, that the actor had evil intent and took some action toward achieving his or her purpose. For example, suppose that Lloyd attempts to kill Susie by putting a fatal dose of poison in her beer. Fortunately, Susie decides she would rather have orange juice and pours the beer out. Susie has not been harmed in any way. Nevertheless, Lloyd may be held liable for attempted murder. It is important to note that there would be no civil liability under these circumstances, as no injury was actually produced. That criminal law punishes attempts whereas civil law does not exemplifies the special concern of the criminal law with immoral purpose.

The Problems Posed by Strict and Vicarious Liability

Like the principle of "public harm," the "evil-meaning actor" principle has significant exceptions as well. Criminal law is often employed to penalize those who lack any evil intent. This is apparent in the so-called *strict liability offenses*, which impose criminal sanctions for acts without regard to the actor's purpose. The act itself constitutes the crime. Intentions are immaterial. For example, it has long been the case in many jurisdictions that an adult who engages in consensual sexual relations with a minor may be held criminally liable for statutory rape even if the child claimed to be an adult and the adult honestly believed that the child had reached the age of majority. Similarly, in many jurisdictions the crime of bigamy is a strict liability offense. Even if one marries a second spouse in the mistaken but honest belief that one's former spouse is dead or that one's former spouse has obtained a lawful divorce, one's action in entering the second marriage can constitute grounds for criminal liability.

In recent years there has been a proliferation of strict liability statutes. Strict liability for one's own conduct also has been supplemented by the notion of *vicarious liability*, which permits the state to hold employers criminally liable for the actions of their employees. Common examples of strict liability offenses include the sale of misbranded, impure, or adulterated food and drugs; the sale of liquor to underage or intoxicated persons; and violations of traffic regulations, motor vehicle laws, child labor laws, building codes, and air and water pollution standards. These developments have stirred considerable controversy. A fundamental postulate of the criminal law is violated by the passage and enforcement of such legislation. In the words of Justice Holmes (1881: 3): "Even a dog distinguishes between being stumbled over and being kicked." The ends of justice seldom are served when a criminal sanction is applied where a harm done is unaccompanied by mental fault, where the offender neither intended to do harm nor consciously disregarded a risk of harm, and, indeed, where the offender may have exercised the utmost care to see that no harm was done.

The factors that encouraged the creation of strict liability statutes were described by Justice Jackson in his opinion for the majority in *Morrisette v. United States*:

[There is] a century-old but accelerating tendency . . . to call into existence new duties and crimes which disregard any ingredient of intent. The industrial revolution multiplied the number of workmen exposed to injury from increasingly powerful and complex mechanisms, driven by freshly discovered sources of energy, requiring higher precautions by employers. Traffic of velocities, volumes and varieties unheard of, came to subject the wayfarer to intolerable casualty risks if owners and drivers were not to observe new cares and uniformities of conduct. Congestion of cities and crowding of quarters called for health and welfare regulations undreamed of in simpler times. Wide distribution of goods became an instrument of wide distribution of harm when those who dispersed food, drink, drugs, and even securities, did not comply with reasonable standards of quality, integrity, disclosure and care. Such dangers have engendered increasingly numerous and detailed regulations which heighten the duties of those in control of particular industries, trades, properties or activities that affect public health, safety or welfare [342 U.S. 246, 252 (1952)].

The uses (or abuses) to which strict liability statutes have been put include the following:

A bar owner was held criminally liable after one of his employee's served liquor to an underage customer. The employer was unaware of the employee's action, was not present when it took place, and had given the employee strict instructions to the contrary [*Commonwealth v. Koczwara* 395 Pa. 575 (1959)].

A shipping officer was convicted of distributing adulterated drugs after he received drugs from a pharmaceutical firm and, without knowing that they were impure, delivered them to physicians [*United States v. Dotterweich*, 320 U.S. 277 (1943)].

An air pollution control officer was held criminally liable when it was found that the company for which he worked had exceeded tolerable air pollution standards. The conviction was upheld despite the fact that the officer had purchased and installed air pollution equipment and had taken precautions to avoid pollution [*State v. Arizona Mines Supply Co.*, 107 Ariz. 199 (1971)].

A number of justifications have been offered for dispensing with the requirement of moral culpability. Most focus on issues of expediency. First, it is frequently argued that at least some of the harms that strict liability statutes aim to prevent are so serious (for example, contamination of air and water) as to warrant the most stringent methods of control. Strict liability statutes are said to encourage people to be more careful, and this benefit is thought to outweigh the potential risk of convicting innocent-minded people (for instance, Mix [1968] and Wasserstrom [1960].

Second, especially when the acts of corporations produce harm, supporters argue that it is very difficult to prove intent. The claim is that regulatory offenses might as well be stricken from the books were a showing of intent to be required.

Third, with regard to violations of traffic regulations and motor vehicle laws, it is argued that these offenses occur in such great numbers that courts would become overburdened, prosecutors would encounter major obstacles, and offenders would fabricate fraudulent defenses if a showing of intent were required (Mueller, 1955: 38-39).

Finally, it is suggested that even though strict liability offenses are labelled criminal, they are really only civil or "quasicriminal" because conviction generally results only in the imposition of a fine.

A growing number of critics remain unpersuaded by these arguments. To them, strict liability represents a clear abuse of the law making process. Whereas criminal liability might be imposed when an individual should have known that his conduct would produce the harm prohibited by law (that is, negligent acts), strict liability provisions are said to insist upon knowledge of what could not be known and consequently are neither necessary nor just (Perkins and Boyce, 1982: 905; Mueller, 1955; Packer, 1962: 109). In addition, critics claim that when attributions of blame are based on accidental wrongdoing, public confidence in both the justice system and the law is undermined and the force of the criminal sanction is diluted (see, for instance, Hart, 1958). Finally, critics point out that, were these strict liability offenses merely civil, it would follow that they should be removed from the criminal courts. That they are not merely civil offenses is clear from the fact that liability is not restricted to fines. Some strict liability offenses carry potential penalties of forfeiture of property, suspension of licenses, probation, and even terms of incarceration (for example, *In re Marley*, 29 Cal. 2d 525 [1946]).

THE NATURE OF THE CRIMINAL SANCTION

We turn our attention now to the question of whether there is something distinctive about the nature of the criminal sanction. In a famous essay, Hart (1958) maintains that the principal if not the only differentiating feature of the criminal law is that only criminal sanctions are both accompanied by and justified by the condemnation of the community. To support his contention, Hart cites Gardner (1953: 193):

> The essence of punishment for moral delinquency lies in the criminal conviction itself. One may lose more money in the stock market than in a court-room; a prisoner of war camp may well provide a harsher environment than a state prison; death on the field of battle has the same physical characteristics as death by sentence of law. It is the expression of the community's hatred, fear, or contempt for the convict which alone characterizes physical hardship as punishment.

As with other differences between criminal and civil law, this distinction has some merit. There is a stigma that attaches to a criminal conviction—quite apart from any punishment that may follow—that is generally not found with civil judgments. If we reflect for a moment on the different terminology that we employ in criminal and civil cases, we see that Hart's argument has some validity. The criminal court makes determinations of "guilt" that result in "conviction," and the defendant, once convicted, is "sentenced." To find an individual "guilty" of a crime implies moral blameworthiness, while the word "convict," especially its noun form, carries considerable stigma. Civil courts, in contrast, make "findings" that result in "judgments." The defendant in a civil case against whom the judgment is entered is simply the loser of the suit who may be ordered to pay "damages." The terminology used in the civil law system is not nearly so "value-loaded" as the language we use in criminal cases.

In former times Hart's argument would have been especially persuasive. In the early days of common law those few forms of conduct that were recognized as crimes were serious *mala in se* offenses. However, the reach of the criminal law has expanded enormously. Hart was not unaware of this development. He commented upon the unfortunate tendency of modern criminal statutes to penalize persons who are not morally blameworthy and considered this to be an abuse because "a criminal conviction carries with it an ineradicable connotation of moral condemnation" (Hart, 1958: 424).

Hart's position notwithstanding, it is clear that public condemnation is not always inherent in a criminal conviction. For example, every day hundreds of persons are convicted of reckless driving. One would be hard pressed to maintain that they are all targets of community condemnation. Indeed, given the highly urbanized, heterogeneous society that we live in, it is doubtful that any but the most heinous of crimes even results in community awareness. Probably the same can be said of civil judgments. Most go unattended. But occasionally even civil suits provoke strong public sentiments of condemnation. Consider public reaction to the Ford Motor Company during the 1970s after it was revealed that the company had manufactured and distributed the Pinto despite known dangers in the car's fuel system that resulted in approximately 100 deaths and many more injuries. Or consider the reaction to A. H. Robbins Company's development and marketing of the Dalkon Shield, a contraceptive device that was responsible for numerous deaths, hysterectomies, and uterine infections.

Another distinction sometimes made between the criminal and the civil sanction is that the purpose of the former is punitive whereas the goal of the latter is compensatory (see, for instance, Bassiouni, 1978). In theory, this is correct. For example, retributive themes abound in criminal law but are generally absent from discussions of the civil law. However, in practice the distinction is less clear. The most common criminal sanctions are probation, fines, and incarceration. Each is said to serve some goal of punishment. Nevertheless, there have been times, especially during the first six decades of this century, when the prevailing ideology underlying the use of these methods was rehabilitative rather than punitive. In addition, victim restitution, a sanction that is clearly compensatory, is regularly ordered by our criminal courts.

On the civil side, the system is predominantly compensatory, but it is by no means entirely so. Quite frequently exemplary or punitive damages are ordered. They involve payments over and above what would be required to compensate the injury. The clear intent of these payments is to punish the wrongdoer and to deter others from similar violations.

When we turn our attentions away from the justifications given for imposing criminal and civil sanctions and look instead at how these sanctions actually are experienced by those upon whom they are imposed, the punitive-compensatory distinction is further weakened. Civil fines may place a real hardship on those ordered to pay them. Moreover, civil incarceration (e.g., institutionalization of the mentally ill, commitment of juvenile delinquents to training schools) involves a severe deprivation of liberty that may be experienced as no less punishing than penal incarceration. Neither the intent of the committing authority nor the civil label attached to the commitment procedure reduces the punitive effect of forced incarceration.

What, then, can be said about the distinctions between criminal and civil law? Some would conclude that there are no real differences in either the scope, the purposes, or the methods used by the two systems and that the only distinctive feature either of the things we call crimes or of the penalties attached to them is that they have been labelled "criminal" by governmental authority. Such a conclusion at least modestly overstates the case. The distinctions noted between the nature of crimes and civil wrongs, between the purposes of criminal and civil law, and between criminal versus civil sanctions, are matters of emphasis or degree. The differentiating principles we have examined are generally true and it would be a mistake to conclude that the existence of overlap and exceptions negates real differences.

THE ELEMENTS OF CRIME

Our aim in this section is to provide an overview of what might be termed the "architecture of the criminal law" (Cohen, 1980). We will discuss four principles of criminal liability that, with some exceptions, constitute the essential components of all crimes. These basic principles relate to the requirements of (1) *a mental state,* (2) *an act,* (3) *concurrence of the mental state and the act, and* (4) *causation.* The specific forms that these elements take of course differ from one crime to another (for example, the mental state involved in first degree murder is distinct from that involved in voluntary manslaughter), but each element is found in nearly every social harm that is defined as crime and made punishable by law.

Mental State

In general it can be said that the reach of the criminal law does not extend to those who act without mental fault. Although there are some notable exceptions to this rule—as in the case of strict liability and vicarious liability offenses—we draw a distinction between intended and unintended acts and attach criminal liability only when intent is present. This prerequisite for criminal liability is deeply rooted in our legal heritage—by the 1600s, judges defined all crimes at common law to include an element of intent—and is expressed in the Latin maxim *"Non facit reum nisi mens sit rea"* (an act does not make a person guilty unless the mind is guilty). This element of a crime is referred to by the term *mens rea.*

Mens rea is a fairly complex concept. On a general level, it refers simply to the mental element of a crime—the actor's state of mind at the time the forbidden act was committed—as distinct from the act itself, which is the material or physical element. *Mens rea* is sometimes equated with intent. Intent, however, should be understood to mean simply a purpose or resolve to commit an act rather than advance planning or prolonged deliberation. A conscious awareness or appreciation of the conduct in which one is engaged may suffice to fulfill the *mens rea* requirement.

The type of mental fault required for criminal liability is not the same for all offenses. For some crimes, it must be shown that the offender acted "with malice aforethought," whereas for others the prosecution is required to prove that the act was committed "knowingly," "willfully," "negligently," "wantonly," or "recklessly." Further, some crimes require only an intent to commit a forbidden act (for example, arson, trespass, rape). Others require an intent to produce a forbidden result (for instance, murder, manslaughter, mayhem).

Mens rea is often confused with motive, and it is important that we distinguish the two concepts at the outset. Motive reflects the reason for the act, the desire that moved the actor to behave in the way he or she did. The law is generally unconcerned with why the actor committed the forbidden act. For example, it matters not whether one kills out of truly evil versus humanitarian and benificent motives (as in some cases involving euthanasia or "mercy killing") as long as there is intent to kill. "The wholly laudable ultimate end sought to be realized by the commission of a crime is rejected by the law if the intent of the actor is to produce certain consequences which are illegal" (Bassiouni, 1978: 171).

The law distinguishes between several analytically distinct levels of *mens rea*. It recognizes that some offenders act with a greater degree of evil intent than others and therefore properly are held to a higher standard of culpability. For example, one who aims an automobile toward another with the specific purpose of striking and killing that other person is held to be more culpable for his or her actions than one who drives an automobile at such an outrageously high rate of speed that it is foreseeable that someone may be killed. As the penal codes of the various states use widely divergent terms to refer to various levels of culpability, we shall confine our discussion here to the four levels of intent recognized by the American Law Institute's very influential *Model Penal Code: purposively, knowingly, recklessly,* and *negligently.*

Crimes Requiring
Purpose and Knowledge

The highest level of culpability recognized by the Model Penal Code involves action made *purposely,* that is, with the "conscious object" either to engage in forbidden conduct or to produce a forbidden result (Model Penal Code, Section 2.02[a]). An example of the former is arson, which at common law was defined as the malicious burning of the dwelling of another. Conscious deliberation to set fire to a dwelling is sufficient to fulfill the *mens rea* requirement no matter what the desired result might be (for instance, destroying a room, destroying the entire house). Murder, on the other hand, is a crime that requires a result-oriented *mens rea.* Unless the defendant acts with the conscious object of producing the death of another, then the *mens rea* element of purposeful killing has not been satisfied.

A slightly lesser degree of culpability is reflected in action that is engaged in *knowingly.* A person acts knowingly when "he is aware that it is practically certain that his conduct will cause a [forbidden] result" or "is aware that his conduct is of [a forbidden] nature" (Model Penal Code, Section 2.02[b]). Thus, when an individual does not desire a particular result but is nevertheless aware that it is almost certain to occur, he or she is said to have acted knowingly. To illustrate, suppose that an individual plants a bomb in the office of an employer by whom he recently has been fired. Although he has no desire to kill any of the other employees who share the office, he knows that the death of these others is an almost certain consequence of his actions. For legal purposes, he will be said to have possessed the intent to kill those others who die when the bomb explodes.

Crimes Requiring
Recklessness and Negligence

A third level of culpability involves *recklessness,* which applies to one who "consciously disregards a substantial and unjustifiable risk of harm to persons or property" and in which the disregard "involves a gross deviation from the standard of conduct that a law-abiding person would observe in the actor's situation" (Model Penal Code, Section 2.02 (2)[c]). To act recklessly, a person must be aware that his or her conduct creates a substantial risk of harm and nonetheless proceed to act with a lack of concern regarding the danger. Recklessness does not require an actual resolve to harm, nor does it require knowledge at the time of the act that a particular harm is likely to result. Awareness that a particular harm *might* result is sufficient (LaFave and Scott, 1972: 216). Probably the most common offense to incorporate this mental element is reckless driving, which is defined in Florida, for example, as driving any vehicle with "wanton and willful disregard for the safety of persons or property" (Florida Statutes Annotated, Section 316.192). Recklessness is the requisite mental element in many personal injury offenses as well. If, for example, one's reckless driving has the consequence of killing a pedestrian, one could be held liable for the crime of manslaughter.

The lowest level of culpability recognized by the Model Penal Code is *negligence.* Negligence occurs when an individual's conduct creates a risk of harm, when (1) the conduct represents "a gross deviation from the standard of care that a reasonable person would observe in the actor's situation" and (2) the individual is unaware, but "should be aware of a substantial and unjustifiable risk" (Model Penal Code, Section 2.02(2)[c]). Negligence is similar to recklessness in that both require that the actor engage in risk-creating conduct that represents a gross deviation from a standard of ordinary or reasonable care. The essential difference between the two lies in the fact that when individuals act recklessly, they are consciously aware of the risk they are creating. Those who act negligently are unaware of that risk. An illustration drawn from one of the leading cases in this area may help to clarify the concept of negligence:

The defendant, in an apparently well-motivated attempt to heal a sick woman, wrapped her body with rags soaked in kerosene, unaware of the dangers involved. The kerosene produced burns that caused the woman's death. The defendant was convicted of manslaughter on the grounds that his behavior created a great risk of which a "reasonable man" would have been aware. (*Commonwealth v. Pierce*, 138 Mass. 165 [1884]).

Being unaware, one who acts negligently has neither any desire to do harm nor any expectation that harm may result. The question arises as to whether it is fair to blame a person for creating a risk of which he or she had no knowledge. Strong objections to negligence statutes have been voiced because, like strict liability statutes, they dispense with the element of mental fault that lies at the core of criminal law theory.

If the defendant, being mistaken as to the material facts, is to be punished because his mistake is one an average man would not make, punishment will sometimes be inflicted when the criminal mind does not exist. Such a result is contrary to fundamental principles, and is plainly unjust, for a man should not be held criminal because of lack of intelligence [Keedy, 1908: 84; See also Hall (1963), and Fletcher (1971)].

Supporters claim that there is mental fault in negligence in that the actor clearly *ought* to have been aware of the risk. Most commonly, however, negligence statutes are defended on wholly pragmatic grounds. Insofar as they encourage people to be more conscious of the risks they take or create, they reduce the incidence of dangerous behavior and promote public safety (LaFave and Scott, 1972; Hall, 1960). Whether civil remedies alone might serve these purposes equally well is an issue of continued debate and controversy.

General Intent, Specific Intent, and Scienter

Different crimes require different levels of intent. In addition, some crimes refer to different *forms* of intent that have important implications for the kinds and amounts of proof of the defendant's mental state that the prosecution must show. For some crimes only general intent is required. This means that the defendant's intent will be presumed from the commission of the crime itself. It is a frequently stated maxim that people are presumed to intend the natural and probable consequences of their acts (*Harrison v. Commonwealth*, 79 Va. 374 [1884]; *Curtis v. State*, 118 Ala. 125 [1897]; *State v. Gilmore*, 320 Ill. 233 [1926]; *State v. Cooper*, 180 Mont. 68 [1979]). Thus, with "general intent" crimes, the intent with which the act was done is inferred from the words and conduct of the defendant and the circumstances surrounding the offense. No specific proof of the defendant's intent is required of the prosecution. The defendant bears the burden of overcoming the presumption of intent by demonstrating its absence.

Specific intent crimes require that the prosecution prove beyond a reasonable doubt the defendant's intent with respect to a particular element of the offense. For example, the crime of burglary is commonly defined to include the elements of (1) the act of entering a building and (2) the specific intent to commit a felony therein. The mere act of entering a building does not support an inference that the defendant entered with the intent to commit burglary. The prosecution must show that the defendant did so with the intent to commit a felony (*Peck v. Dunn*, 574 P.2d 367 [Utah 1978]). Other crimes involving specific intent include larceny (the taking and carrying away of the property of another with intent to steal) and assault with intent to kill.

Another special mental element that must be proven with respect to certain crimes is called *scienter*. Scienter refers to a specific element of knowledge rather than intent or purpose. For example, the crime of receiving stolen property almost always is defined to include knowledge on the part of the defendant that the property received was stolen. Other crimes that ordinarily require proof of the defendant's knowledge of the existence of a particular fact include assault on a law enforcement officer (requiring proof of prior knowledge that the victim was a law enforcement officer) and possession of obscene material (requiring proof of prior knowledge of the nature of the material).

Conduct

Although the mental element is not present in every offense, all crimes require conduct, which is referred to as *actus reus*. The conduct requirement precludes the criminalization of evil thoughts or intentions. This is reflected in the ancient maxim *"Cogitationis peonam nemo patitur"* (No one is punishable for his thoughts). This limitation is commonly justified on such grounds as (1) problems of proof (How can we be certain of the thoughts of another?), (2) difficulties in distinguishing real intent from idle daydreaming, and (3) the notion that the law's business is not to punish those who entertain criminal thoughts but only those who allow those thoughts to control their actions (Perkins and Boyce, 1982: 605). (For further discussion of these and other issues raised by the criminalization of thoughts, see Blackstone, 1778; Goldstein, 1959; and Williams, 1961).

Unlike thoughts, words are considered acts for purposes of the criminal law. For example, it is a federal offense to threaten to kill or to inflict bodily harm on the president (18 U.S.C.A., Section 871(a), 1976). Terroristic threats, harrassing communications, perjury (making a false statement under oath), conspiracy (formulating an agreement with another to commit a crime), and solicitation (commanding, encouraging, hiring, or requesting another to commit a crime), are other common examples of offenses in which words suffice to constitute the *actus reus* element. In addition, possession is dealt with as a special kind of *actus reus*. To be held liable for a possessory crime it generally suffices if the defendant either "knowingly procured or received" the item or "was aware of his control thereof for a sufficient period to have been able to terminate his possession" (*Model Penal Code,* Section 2.01[4]). The defendant need not have legal title to the item to be held criminally liable. It also is not necessary that the item be on his or her person or in his or her immediate control (that is, *actual possession).* It is generally enough if the defendant is in a position to exercise control over the item, such as where it is kept in his or her home or automobile (in other words, *constructive possession).*

Finally, the *actus reus* requirement of criminal law can be satisfied by either (1) an overt act or (2) a failure to act when one has a legal duty to act. In other words, criminal law extends to acts of both commission and omission. A familiar example of an offense of the latter type is failure to file an income tax return. When the law imposes a duty to act, failure to do what the law requires is considered conduct for the purpose of the *actus reus* requirement.

Liability for Overt Acts

When an overt act is the basis for criminal liability, the action must be *voluntary.* The criminal law does not hold people responsible for involuntary conduct, but only for behavior that is "willed" (Holmes, 1881: 51). Were an individual to injure another during an episode of sleepwalking, for example, the law would not hold him or her criminally liable. Other actions that are generally considered to be involuntary for purposes of the criminal law are convulsions, epileptic seizures, reflex actions, and bodily movements made by one individual through force applied by another. For example, if John pushes Carol into Marion and Marion falls off a cliff to her death, Carol will not be held criminally liable. Her act is considered to be involuntary.

However, not every involuntary action that causes harm is beyond the reach of the criminal law. Complications arise when harm-producing involuntary action is preceded by voluntary risk-taking behavior on the part of an individual who is aware of his or her susceptibility to potentially dangerous involuntary bodily movements. Consider, for example, the following case:

> The indictment states essentially that the defendant, knowing that he was subject to epileptic attacks . . . rendering him likely to lose consciousness for a considerable period of time was culpably negligent in that he consciously undertook to and did operate his Buick sedan on a public highway and while so doing suffered such an attack which caused said automobile to travel at a fast and reckless speed, jumping the curb and driving over the sidewalk causing the death of four persons. In our opinion, this clearly states a violation of . . . the penal law . . . [A] person who operates or drives any vehicle of any kind in a reckless or culpably negligent manner, whereby a human being is killed is guilty of criminal negligence in the operation of a vehicle resulting in death. This defendant knew he was subject to epileptic attacks and seizures that might strike at any time. He also knew that a moving vehicle uncontrolled on a public highway is a highly dangerous instrumentality capable of unrestrained destruction. With this knowledge, and without anyone accompanying him, he deliberately took a chance by making a conscious choice of a course of action in disregard of the consequences that he knew might follow from his conscious act, and which in this case did ensue [*People v. Decina,* 2 N.Y. 2d, 133, 139-140 (1956)].

Liability for Omissions

The *actus reus* requirement may be met by a failure to act if and only if one has a *legal* duty to act. A legal duty can be imposed in several ways. First, of course, statutory law may create such an obligation. This is exemplified by such statutes as those that require the filing of income tax returns, the obligation of citizens to assist law enforcement officers under some circumstances, and the duty to provide assistance to those who may have been injured in traffic accidents in which one has been involved.

Second, some categories of persons are said to have a special relationship to other persons, a special relationship that imposes upon them a legal obligation to act. The most obvious illustration of this is the special relationship that is said to exist between parents and their children. Whereas an ordinary citizen would have no legal obligation to protect a child from some obvious threat to his or her safety, the failure of such a child's parents to make a reasonable effort to protect him or her from harm can become the basis for a criminal prosecution.

Third, roughly analogous special relationships can be established by contractual commitments. For instance, doctors, nurses, lifeguards, babysitters, and many others have willingly accepted a responsibility to protect others. Failure to act is not merely a breach of contract. It can be the basis for criminal prosecution.

Finally, and essentially an extension of the previous two points, a legal obligation to act may be imposed on those who have voluntarily assumed the responsibility to care for others. Were you, for instance, to agree to care for the child of a neighbor, the fact that you did so without compensation of any kind (that is, you have no contract to act as a babysitter), then you would be legally obligated to come to the assistance of that child should the need arise. Thus, were the young child to drown in a bathtub while you watched your favorite television program, you might well confront a manslaughter prosecution.

Many European countries impose a legal duty to act upon everyone who is physically able to assist another who is in peril as long as providing such assistance would not endanger the life of the person who assists (for an excellent discussion, see Feldbrugge, 1966: 630). In contrast, it has long been the view in this country that "the need of one and the opportunity of another to be of assistance are not alone sufficient to give rise to a legal duty to take positive action" (Perkins and Boyce, 1982: 662). Thus, a stranger who stands idly by and watches while an intoxicated man passes out in a dimly lit street and is subsequently struck and killed by a car will not be held liable for his failure to pull the man to safety even though he might have done so with relative ease and at little risk to himself. Although we would certainly find such a failure to act *morally* reprehensible, it does not constitute a *legal* wrong. Our criminal law takes a very restrictive view of legal liability for omissions.

[O]ur rule may appear too lenient. But we do not think that it can be made more severe, without disturbing the whole order of society. It is true that the man who, having abundance of wealth, suffers a fellow creature to die of hunger at his feet, is a bad man—a worse man, probably, than many of those for whom we have provided very severe punishment. But we are unable to see where, if we make such a man legally punishable, we can draw the line. If the rich man who refuses to save a beggar's life at the cost of a little copper is a murderer, is the poor man just one degree above beggary also to be a murderer if he omits to invite the beggar to partake his hard earned rice? . . . It is, indeed, most highly desirable that men should not merely abstain from doing harm to their neighbors, but should render active service to their neighbors. In general, however, the penal law must content itself with keeping men from doing positive harm, and must leave to public opinion, and to the teachers of morality and religion, the office of furnishing men with motives for doing positive good. It is evident that to attempt to punish men by law for not rendering to others all the service which it is their [moral] duty to render to others would be preposterous. We must grant immunity to the vast majority of these omissions which a benevolent morality would pronounce reprehensible, and must content ourselves with punishing such omissions only when they are distinguished from the rest by some circumstance which marks them out as peculiarly fit objects of penal legislation [Macauley, 1851: 158-60].

Concurrence

When a crime is defined to require both an act and some element of mental fault, generally the offense will not be said to have been committed unless there is *concurrence* of the *mens rea* and the *actus reus*. In other words, the mental fault must precede the forbidden act. Thus, if we find a mental fault without a forbidden act or a forbidden act without mental fault, then there is no crime (unless of course the offense is one of strict liability). It is also possible to have both a forbidden act and mental fault and still not have a crime. Suppose, for example, that Roberta buys a television set from Sam and later learns that the set was stolen. Roberta decides to keep the television. Here there is both criminal intent and a forbidden act but, because the intent came after rather than before the act, there is no concurrence. The crime of receiving stolen property has not occurred. To be held liable for receiving stolen property, Roberta would have had to possess knowledge that the television was stolen *at the time that she received it.*

With crimes that are defined to prohibit some result (for example, murder, battery, mayhem), it is important to recognize that the requirement of concurrence does not mean that the necessary *mens rea* must continue until the forbidden result occurs. It is necessary only that the mental state activate the conduct that produces the harm. For example, suppose that Frank stabs Peter with an intent to kill him. Peter is taken to the hospital where he remains alive for weeks or even months. Frank becomes remorseful for his actions and prays sincerely that Peter will live. Peter finally dies from his wounds. Although at the time of Peter's death Frank has no criminal intent, he is nonetheless responsible for murder.

The reader should note that there is no problem of concurrence when a person acts with intent to harm one person but harms someone other than the anticipated target. Suppose, for example, that Roger coldly and calculatedly aims a gun at Fred with the intent to kill him. Roger is a poor marksman and the bullet hits and kills Dwayne. May Roger be held liable for murder? Yes. Roger shot and killed (the *actus reus* required for murder) in a premeditated fashion (the *mens rea* required for murder). He is thus properly held liable for murder regardless of the fact that his conduct caused the death of someone other than his intended victim. This is sometimes referred to as the *doctrine of transferred intent* (in other words, the intent to injure one person is said to be transferred to another should the actual victim be other than the person intended). This doctrine applies to nonpersonal injury cases as well. Transferred intent would apply, for example, to a case in which a person set a fire with the intent to destroy one building, but in which the wind caused the fire to spread to an adjacent building instead. The doctrine of transferred intent does have important limitations. For example, it does not apply when an individual has the requisite *mens rea* for one type of offense but commits an act that requires a different *mens rea*. A leading case that illustrates this requirement involved a sailor who went to the hold of a ship with the intent to steal some rum. He lit a match to see better and the rum caught fire, completely destroying the ship. Because his intent related to one type of harm (theft) while the harm that resulted required a different mental state (intent to burn), he was not held liable for arson [*Regina v. Faulkner*, 13 Cox C.C. 550 (1877)]. (Of course, had he been found to have acted recklessly or negligently in lighting the match, he might have been criminally liable.) Generally, when an individual has *mens rea* requisite for one type of crime but the behavior in which he engages requires a different type of *mens rea*, the defendant will not be held criminally liable. Significant exceptions to this statement are found in the felony-murder and misdemeanor-manslaughter rules.

The Felony-Murder and Misdemeanor-Manslaughter Rules

Although it is ordinarily the case that persons may not be held criminally liable for their actions unless there is a concurrence of the *actus reus* and the *mens rea*, the *felony-murder* and *misdemeanor-manslaughter doctrines* constitute important exceptions to this rule. The felony-murder rule holds that a killing that occurs during the perpetration of a felony constitutes a murder (usually a murder in the first degree). The misdemeanor-manslaughter rule holds that a killing that occurs during the perpetration of a misdemeanor constitutes manslaughter. What is perhaps most significant about these rules is that they hold offenders liable for killings that may be entirely unintentional. A few examples should suffice to illustrate their operation.

A robber held up an individual at gunpoint and, quite accidentally, the gun went off, killing the victim. Although the killing was unintentional, the offender was held liable for first degree murder [*Commonwealth v. McManus*, 282 Pa. 25 (1925); *McCutcheon v. State*, 199 Ind. 247 (1927); *Simpson v. Wainwright*, 439 F. 2d 948 (5th Cir. 1971)].

An individual intentionally set fire to a building. He was subsequently convicted of first degree murder after a fireman was killed fighting the blaze [*State v. Glover*, 330 Mo. 709 (1932)].

A robber was held liable for first degree murder when a victim became so upset that he died of a heart attack during the commission of the robbery [*State v. McKeiver*, 213 A. 2d 320 (1965); *People v. Stamp*, 2 Cal. App. 3d 203 (1970)].

Seven men together committed a robbery. During the robbery, one of the robbers became angry with one of his accomplices and shot and killed him. The six surviving robbers were all convicted of murder, including the accomplice that was waiting outside in the getaway car [*People v. Cabaltero*, 31 Cal. App. 2d (1939)].

A fleeing burglar was held liable for murder when a police officer who was attempting to apprehend him mistakenly shot a fellow officer [*People v. Hickman*, 59 Ill.2d 89 (1974)].

These illustrations quite obviously differ in some important regards. In the first three, for instance, all of us would recognize that there is an offender who was engaging in criminal behavior that, albeit in the absence of any malice, resulted in the death of another person. In the last two examples, we encounter people being held liable for murder even though they neither intended to take a human life nor in fact personally took a human life. Under the felony-murder and misdemeanor-manslaughter rules, however, such distinctions are largely irrelevant. Each of these defendants was involved in felonious conduct and human lives were lost as a direct consequence of that conduct.

Obviously, the felony-murder and misdemeanor-manslaughter rules are especially advantageous to the prosecution. All that need be demonstrated is the intent to commit the underlying felony or misdemeanor. As long as the killing is causally related to the perpetration of this other crime, invocation of either the felony-murder or the misdemeanor-manslaughter rule will result in the offender being held strictly liable for the death. Further, if there are accomplices to the crime, the rule will be extended to them through the principle of vicarious liability based on their participation in the crime.

The felony-murder rule was created early in the development of common law at a time when all felonies were punishable by death. Thus, no greater punishment was imposed for the killing than was applied to the underlying felony that the offender intended to commit. Over the years, however, the scope of the rule was expanded. Its initial extension was to violent and forcible felonies not punishable by death. The rationale for this extension was that because such crimes are inherently dangerous to life and limb, their commission creates a foreseeable risk of the death of others, for which the offender may properly be held criminally liable (Holmes, 1881: 59). The purpose of the rule was to deter offenders from committing crimes that carry a high risk of death by holding them strictly liable for even accidental killings that they might commit during the perpetration of one of these offenses. In the early part of this century, the felony-murder and misdemeanor-manslaughter rules were extended far beyond their previous limits. In some jurisdictions an offender could be held criminally liable for deaths caused in the commission of *any* felony or misdemeanor. Further, they were extended to any killing that occurred during the perpetration of the crime, irrespective of whether the killing was committed by the offender, a victim, a witness, or a police officer. Given the underlying rationale for the felony-murder rule, this is most inappropriate.

Fortunately, most courts have refused to extend the rule to nondangerous offenses even when there is statutory authorization to do so (see, for instance, *People v. Pavlic*, 227 Mich. 562 [1924] and *People v. Henderson*, 19 Cal. 3d 86 [1977]). The recent tendency has been to restrict the applicability of the felony-murder rule to killings that occur during the commission of an inherently dangerous felony (for example, rape, kidnapping, robbery, and other forcible felonies) and to apply the misdemeanor-manslaughter rule only to misdemeanors of the *mala in se* type. However, the rule is still regularly applied when a victim, a witness, or a police officer rather than the offender has caused a death. In addition, accomplices continue to be held vicariously liable for both the deaths of their confederates and deaths caused by their confederates.

Causation

Many crimes include as part of their definitions an element of resultant harm. Examples include homicide (requiring killing), aggravated battery (requiring serious bodily injury), and maiming (requiring disfigurement). In these result-oriented offenses, a crime will not be said to have been committed unless there is a legally recognized causal connection between the offender's actions and the proscribed harm. Usually, causation is easily determined. Mary aims a gun at George's chest, pulls the trigger, and George dies instantly. There can be little doubt about a causal connection between Mary's act and George's death. If this act were committed without justification, defense, or excuse, Mary would certainly be held liable for homicide. Unfortunately, cases arise in which the issue of causation is both complex and difficult. Commonly, for example, other events intervene between the proscribed conduct and the subsequent harm. Suppose, for example, that Mary only manages to inflict a serious wound and George is taken to the hospital where tubes are inserted into his windpipe to maintain his breathing. At first George appears to be recovering nicely. However, after a few days he becomes delirious, pulls out the tubes, and dies (*United States v. Hamilton*, 182 F. Supp. 548 [D.D.C. 1960]); or suppose that while in the hospital George catches a fatal case of scarlet fever from the physician who treats him (*Bush v. Commonwealth*, 78 Ky. 268 [1880]); or suppose that George dies because a physician negligently administers drugs to which George is known to be intolerant (*Rex v. Jordan*, 40 Crim. App. 152 [1956]). Is Mary still liable for murder? To begin to answer questions such as these, we need to delve into some fairly complex rules created to deal with matters of causation.

In order for a causal connection to be established between conduct and a result, the conduct must be both the *actual cause* (the "cause in fact") and the *proximate cause* (legal cause) of the result. The concept of actual causation is often expressed in terms of the "but for" test (that is, the harm would not have occurred but for the actions of the defendant). In each of the examples given above, Mary's conduct constitutes a "but for" cause of George's death. In the first example, Mary's actions were the sole and direct cause of George's death and it is readily apparent that but for Mary's actions, George would have remained alive. When other events intervened between Mary's actions and George's death, the "but for" standard also is met. Had it not been for Mary's action, George would not have been in the hospital to pull out his tubes, contract scarlet fever, or be treated by an incompetent physician.

In order to satisfy the causation requirement for criminal liability, it is necessary *but not sufficient* that an individual's action be an actual cause of a proscribed harm. A cause also must constitute a *proximate cause*. The term "proximate" refers to nearness in causal relation. It expresses the law's concern with those antecedent factors that are closely connected with a particular result.

One very clear standard of proximate causation that traditionally has been applied to homicide cases is the *year and a day rule*, which holds that a person cannot be held to have caused the death of another if the death occurs more than a year and a day after the harm was inflicted. This ancient rule apparently was created because prior to the development of modern medicine it was difficult to determine the precise cause of death. If death occured fairly shortly after an injury was inflicted, it was presumed to be due to the injury. If it occurred some time later, it was plausible to attribute the death to natural causes. Both because the cause of death can be ascertained with great precision and because it is possible to keep people alive through artificial supports for lengthy periods of time, this rule makes little sense today. Still, many jurisdictions have retained it.

Most of the other rules that have been developed to define proximate cause are guides rather than strict rules that can be applied mechanically. We shall examine several of them here. Woven through the situations and illustrations presented below, one should be able to discern that an act generally will not be recognized as the proximate cause of a particular result if (1) the act did not constitute a substantial factor in producing the harm or (2) the harm was due to intervening events that a reasonable person could not have foreseen.

First of all, causation issues frequently arise when the harm results in a manner that was unintended. For example, suppose that Harry shoots Arthur with an intent to kill, but he manages to inflict only a superficial wound. Unknown to Harry, Arthur has a preexisting disease that renders him highly vulnerable to even a minor injury. Arthur dies. What is the nature of Harry's criminal liability? Harry's actions will be ruled the proximate cause of Arthur's death and, if he acted without justification, defense, or excuse, he will be held liable for murder. It is frequently stated that an assailant "takes his victim as he finds him" and is criminally liable if death should occur due to a preexisting weakness. The law views as foreseeable the possibility that a victim may be particularly susceptible to injury.

Second, sometimes natural events intervene between the act and a resulting harm. For example, suppose a wound that would not otherwise have been fatal becomes infected and death results. Is the person who inflicted such a wound liable for the unlawful death? Yes. The infection caused the death, but the act that produced the wound will be recognized as the proximate cause of death. Such an event is a foreseeable consequence of the assailant's actions, and he or she will be held liable for the ultimate harm. However, this situation should be distinguished from one in which the victim is exposed to some other natural cause of death that is entirely unforeseeable. A battery victim lying in a hospital may die after coincidentally contracting a new disease (*Bush v. Commonwealth*, 78 Ky. 268 [1880]). An assault victim left in a field may be struck by lightning. When such an unforeseeable force intervenes to cause the ultimate result, the initial act of harm will not be viewed as a proximate cause of that result. Any intervening event that serves to break the chain of causation between the wrongdoer's action and the resulting harm is often termed a *superseding cause*. However, it is generally held that individuals are responsible for harms that occur as a result of intervening actions of their victims. Consider the following:

A husband threatened to kill his wife with a deadly weapon and, in an effort to escape, she leapt from an upstairs window and fell to her death [*Whiteside v. State*, 115 Tex. Cr. R. 274 (1930)].

A prankster, intending only to have a little fun, fired a gun into the water next to a boat in which several boys were floating. One boy jumped out in fear, which caused the boat to overturn, and two boys drowned [*Letner v. State*, 156 Tenn. 68 (1927)].

In instances such as these in which a victim is killed or injured as a result of impulsive behavior to avoid harm that is both normal and foreseeable, courts generally have not hesitated to find a causal connection between the assailant's acts and the ultimate harm. Other harms resulting from actions taken by victims may similarly be attributed to the assailant. For example, a victim's refusal to seek medical treatment will not exempt the assailant from criminal liability for the victim's death (*State v. Edgerton*, 100 Iowa 63 [1896]; *Bailey v. State*, 22 Ala. App. 185 [1927]; *State v. Johnson*, 36 Del. 341 [1934]; *Commonwealth v. Hackett*, 84 Mass. 136 [1861]). And when the injury inflicted by an assailant has caused the victim to become so distraught and irresponsible as to commit suicide, the conduct of the assailant has been held to be the cause of the victim's death (*Stephenson v. State*, 205 Ind. 141 [1932]; *People v. Lewis*, 124 Cal. 551 [1899]; *Commonwealth v. Wright*, 455 Pa. 480 [1974]).

Under certain circumstances, intervening acts of third persons may break the chain of causation. If an assault victim dies as a result of unskilled or even negligent medical care, the act of the assailant is generally held to be the proximate cause of death (*Johnson v. State*, 64 Fla. 321 [1912]; *Thomas v. State*, 139 Ala. 80 [1904]; *Crews v. State*, 44 Ga. App. 546 [1932]; *Commonwealth v. Hackett*, 84 Mass. 136 [1861]; *State v. Rueckert*, 221 Kan. 727 [1977]). However, if the victim dies as a result of "grossly negligent" treatment, especially when the injury itself is minor, the action of medical personnel will generally be viewed as a superseding cause (*Parsons v. State*, 21 Ala. 300 [1852]; *State v. Morphy*, 33 Iowa 270 [1871]; *People v. Cook*, 39 Mich. 236 [1878]; *McDaniel v. State*, 76 Ala. 1 [1884]). The distinction between the two results seems to lie in the view that ordinary negligence on the part of a physician is foreseeable, whereas gross negligence is unforeseeable.

Whether or not the harm produced by a third party will be deemed to be a superseding cause depends in large measure on the foreseeability of the intervening events. Thus, when an assailant left an individual lying unconscious on a roadway at night and the victim was subsequently struck by a car and killed, the action of the driver of the vehicle, being foreseeable, was not deemed superseding and the assailant was held liable for homicide (*People v. Fowler*, 178 Cal. 657 [1918]). However, when an individual knocked someone down and a third person subsequently kicked the victim in the head producing death, the first assailant was not held criminally liable. The conduct of the third party was an unforeseeable intervening cause (*Lewis v. Commonwealth*, 19 Ky. L. Rep. 1139 [1897]. See also *State v. Scates*, 50 N.C. 420 [1858]; *Walker v. State*, 116 Ga. 537 [1902]; *State v. Wood*, 53 Vt. 560 [1881]).

SUMMARY

We have covered a good deal of ground in this chapter. We began with an attempt to outline the broad contours of criminal law. In this process we identified criminal law as a subfield of public law and attempted to isolate the characteristic features of criminal law that distinguish it from civil law. We have seen that, at least as a matter of theory, criminal law seeks to control different kinds of behavior than does civil law, it has different purposes than the civil law, and it utilizes different methods of sanctioning that the civil law. We also have learned that criminal law is concerned only with public harms, that its reach is generally restricted to voluntary and intentional acts committed by morally culpable actors, and that it employs punishment and moral condemnation of the offender as methods of sanctioning. However, we have noted that behind this external facade, these characteristic features of criminal law theory tend to become blurred in actual practice by a number of exceptions.

In this chapter we also have mapped out the essential elements of the things we call crimes. In order for an individual to be convicted of a crime, he or she must have either committed an overt act or failed to act when there was a legal duty to act. This requirement of the criminal law, found in all offenses, refers specifically to acts that are "willed." The act requirement excludes from criminal liability both involuntary conduct and mere thoughts. Another essential element—found in all but strict liability offenses—is the requirement of mental fault or *mens rea*. Because criminal law is most interested in punishing those who are morally culpable, a forbidden act (or a failure to act) must be accompanied by mental fault in order to constitute a crime. The mental fault may consist of an intent purposely or knowingly to produce a prohibited result or to engage in proscribed conduct, or it may consist of a reckless or negligent disregard of a grave risk of harm. Further, we reviewed the requirement of concurrence between the mental state and the act. Unless the mental fault gives rise to the forbidden conduct, no crime has been committed.

Finally, we explored the requirement of causation. For result-oriented offenses, criminal law requires that there be an intimate causal connection between the act and the resultant harm. There must be *both* cause in fact *and* proximate causation. If the connection between an act and a subsequent harm is sufficiently remote, or if unforeseeable intervening circumstances produce the harm, the act will not be said to have caused the harm. In general, criminal law is reluctant to punish individuals whose actions produce results that could not reasonably have been anticipated.

DISCUSSION QUESTIONS

1. Several commentators have suggested that the American law of crimes ought to take a much broader view of criminal liability for omissions in order to bring the legal duty to act into closer conformity with the moral duty to act. European penal codes commonly impose a much more general obligation to provide aid to those in peril. The German penal code provides that:

> Anybody who does not render aid in an accident or common danger or in an emergency situation, although aid is needed and under the circumstances can be expected of him, especially if he would not subject himself thereby to any considerable danger, or if he would not thereby violate other important duties, shall be punished by imprisonment not to exceed one year or a fine [German Penal Code, Section 330(c)].

What benefits and problems do you see with such an approach?

2. What is it about sale of adulterated food, sale of intoxicating beverages to minors, and violation of traffic regulations that justifies a departure from the proposition that criminal liability should be reserved for the morally culpable?

3

THEORIES OF LAW AND
ITS PURPOSES

Until now our attention has focused on the historical development of
our legal tradition, contemporary sources of criminal law, and basic
distinctions that need to be made between subdivisions of both criminal
and noncriminal law. Far too little attention has been devoted to the
considerable bodies of literature that address two fundamental questions. First, what are the social and political origins of law? Is law, for
instance, most accurately thought of as a formalization or codification
of the customs, values, and moral standards of a people? Or is it better
conceptualized as a practical and powerful means by which the
particular interests of a few are protected? Second, and quite apart from
whether law serves the interests of some or all, precisely what is it that we
seek to achieve in the area of criminal law when punishment is imposed
on those who are found guilty by our criminal courts? Is our primary
objective, for example, to assure that offenders "get what they deserve"?
Or is punishment largely a way that we seek to prevent crime through
deterrence or through the involvement of offenders in various types of
rehabilitative programs?

We cannot avoid these critically important concerns any longer. To
address them we will divide this chapter into two fairly independent
parts. In the first we will review and evaluate four basic theories of the
origins of law: the *natural law model*, the *moral consensus model*, the
class conflict model, and the *interest group conflict*. Such theories of law
are of central importance to those criminologists and legal scholars
whose special concerns are with what is loosely referred to as the
sociology of law. We will then turn our attention to a consideration of
three basic perspectives on the purposes of punishment—*retribution,
crime prevention through deterrence and incapacitation*, and *rehabilitation*. Each is commonly employed to provide a moral or ethical
justification for the right of the state impose punishment on those

convicted of criminal acts. This second portion of the chapter will involve us at least as much with the world of moral philosophy as with the subject matter of substantive criminal law.

THE ORIGINS OF LAW:
LAW FROM WHOM? LAW FOR WHOM?

The Natural Law Model

With regard to the natural law model there is relatively little that needs to be said here (but see Fuller, 1964). Whether the notion of natural law is approached from a sacred or a secular vantage point, the basic thesis is that all law either has been or should be derived from certain universal distinctions between good and evil that transcend the limitations of space, time, and cultural differences. Laws lacking such a lofty foundation in the realm of immutable truths are said to have no legitimacy. They would be seen as nonlaws. Consequently, violations of them, although perhaps being met by harsh sanctions imposed by the state, would not be blameworthy in any moral or ethical sense.

The general thought is pleasing enough. One can certainly find abundant historical and contemporary illustrations, for example, of persons engaging in what was or is defined as criminal conduct with the simple and straightforward defense that the law violated was itself in violation of what is here described as natural law. On the other hand, in the sometimes bloody conflicts we have witnessed between feudal lords and serfs, kings and subjects, masters and slaves, and many more, we find each being able to lay what each took to be an equally convincing claim that acts of domination as well as reactions to oppression had a firm attachment to "self-evident" principles of natural law.

The problem, of course, is that we lack any clear and objective way of distinguishing between such claims apart from applying our own value judgments. Those judgments vary widely from person to person, place to place, time to time, and so on. Thus, it is hard to disagree with Ingber's (1981: 321) recent critique of the natural law model:

> The content of natural law consists of whatever the individual ascribing to it desires to advocate. Supporters of both the status quo and radical change have repeatedly invoked it to reach opposite results. Essentially, natural law serves as a debater's bludgeon used to support and defend one's own position while battering those of one's opponents.

Naturally, care should be taken to avoid reading more into our criticism than we intend. For example, we are in no way suggesting that one cannot find any principled way of objecting to racism, sexism, and various other forms of exploitation and oppression. We are saying that those principles must flow logically from the premises one advances regarding, among other possibilities, the value of equality of treatment under law. Such assertions are so fundamental that their validity can be neither proven nor falsified, but our inability to establish their validity does not deprive them of meaning. Thus, it is simply not necessary to advance some claim that their value can be derived from the "black box" of natural law. They do not require some mystical means of being legitimated. One either accepts their value as being self-evident or one rejects them in favor of some alternative set of premises.

Law as an Expression of Moral Consensus

The position advanced by those who see law as little more than a formalization and codification of preexisting norms, values, and customs is only somewhat more difficult to dismiss. To begin with, we earlier distinguished between the *mala in se* and *mala prohibita* categories of criminal law. The former includes offenses believed to be moral wrongs that are "evil in and of themselves." The latter includes acts said to be wrong because of legislative enactments that are premised on concerns other than prevailing moral standards. Approached on quite a general level, it would appear that the consensus model has something to say with regard to the origins of *mala in se* offenses, but it is of less relevance in the case of *mala prohibita* offenses. (Even here, however, one encounters some conceptual/definitional problems in the sense that an offense fitting into the *malum prohibitum* category when it was enacted into law may come to have many if not all of the attributes of a *malum in se* offense if it remains in force over time.)

For instance, such offenses as murder, rape, battery, robbery, and larceny are quite clearly thought of as being harmful and blameworthy for reasons other than their having been defined as crimes. Furthermore, to enact a criminal law regarding which there was wide-spread public opposition and to which substantial numbers of citizens attributed no legitimacy would be foolhardy (see, for example, Hagan, 1980). Efforts during the Prohibition Era to control the manufacture, distribution, and use of alcoholic beverages is an obvious illustration of such a futile effort to exercise the law-making powers of the state. So, too, are those provisions of criminal law that seek to regulate forms of sexual expression that take place between consenting adults. If such laws accomplish any purpose, then the purpose is limited to satisfying the desires of an interest group that seeks to gain some symbolic support for its values even if that type of support has no influence whatsoever on the frequency of the behavior to which it objects. Unfortunately, such symbolic uses of criminal law have a dark side in the obvious sense that some people run the risk of confronting criminal prosecutions and, perhaps more importantly, in the less obvious sense that law enforcement officials are virtually invited to shield arbitrary or discriminatory abuses of their discretionary powers by claiming that they are "just doing their jobs."

Notwithstanding some general validity of the claims advanced by consensus theorists, it is undeniable that their position crumbles when subjected to scrutiny by a less general type of analysis. True, preexisting consensus may give rise to some types of criminal law. Such a broad consensus may be necessary if public perceptions of the legitimacy of law are to be preserved. But a criminal law is not a general requirement to take or refrain from taking action. In our system of criminal law much significance is attached to what is often called the *principle of specificity*. Essentially, it is this principle that requires that law, most especially criminal law, be quite precise in its definition of the conduct it requires or prohibits.

The point is well illustrated by the classic case of *McBoyle v. United States*, 283 U.S. 25 (1931). McBoyle was convicted under a provision of federal law that described as a felony offense the transporting or causing to be transported in interstate or foreign commerce of any stolen motor vehicle. The applicable federal statute defined a motor vehicle as "an automobile, automobile truck, automobile wagon, motorcycle, or any other self-propelled vehicle not designed for running on rails . . . " McBoyle was said to have violated this law by unlawfully transporting an airplane from Illinois to Oklahoma.

On the face of it, McBoyle seems to have gotten himself into big trouble. But had he? Did this federal statute state in sufficiently precise language that the interstate transportation of stolen airplanes was unlawful? The United States Supreme Court did not think that it had. Writing for the majority of the Court, Justice Holmes observed that:

> it is reasonable that a fair warning should be given to the world in language that the common world will understand, of what the law intends to do if a certain line is crossed. To make the warning fair, so far as possible the line should be clear. When a rule of conduct is laid down in words that evoke in the common mind only the picture of vehicles moving on land, the statute should not be extended to aircraft . . . because it might seem to us that similar policy applies . . . or upon the speculation that, if

the legislature had thought of it, very likely broader words would have been used.

There is more to *McBoyle* than a cute illustration of how law sometimes fails to keep abreast of new technology. The real point is that the specific content of particular provisions of law are almost never derived from some sweeping societal consensus. Instead, those specifics are most commonly hammered out in a legislative arena within which efforts are made to advance conflicting claims (for a general overview of relevant research see Black, 1976; Hagan, 1980; Chambliss and Seidman, 1982; and Thomas and Hepburn, 1983). This is most obviously true when the appeal of or opposition to a given law is linked to some organized constituency, but it is really no less true regarding such "obviously" *mala in se* offenses as murder. Deliberations regarding the particular types of murder that deserve to be subjected to the possibility of the death sentence versus a maximum sentence of life imprisonment, for example, are often quite heated. So, too, are debates about what the law will permit as defenses in murder prosecutions. How should the right of citizens to use lethal force be defined? Under what circumstances and with what definitions will an insanity defense prevail? In these and other very crucial areas we find that there is nothing self-evident about criminal law even as it applies to persons who have taken the lives of others.

Class Conflict Theories of Law

At some extreme and opposite end of the continuum on which we find theories of law-making processes is the class conflict model. More or less derived from the works of such major historical figures as Karl Marx and Friedrich Engels, law of all types has been depicted as a tool used by the powerful (that is, the bourgeoisie) in their continuing efforts to exploit the powerless (in other words, the proletariat). The initial focus of such a perspective, of course, is on how a given set of economic and social relationships gives rise to both the state and the body of law it creates. Because the very existence of the ruling class in a capitalist society is said to depend on its ability to exploit the labor potential of workers—the "theory of surplus labor value"—there is said to be an inherent state of mutual antagonism and potential for conflict.

Chaos and revolution, however, can be avoided, or at least delayed, if something of a buffer is erected between these opposing groups. Ideally, if only from the vantage point of the ruling class, the buffer would consist of a set of ideas and institutions that would appear to be legitimate, neutral, and unbiased. The state is said to be such an institution. Marx and Engels (1973: 110-111), for instance, once remarked that "the executive of the modern state is but a committee for managing the common affairs of the whole bourgeoisie." Similarly, Engels contended that any society divided into two opposing classes "needs the state, that means an organisation of the exploiting class for maintaining the external conditions of its production, especially for holding down by force the exploited class" (Engels quoted in Kelsen, 1980: 92). Much the same is said by many Marxists about such legal concepts as "fundamental fairness," "due process of law," and many others that convey the image that law is a neutral set of rules that is somehow detached from the economic and political realities of everyday existence.

Contemporary Marxists, who often refer to themselves as "structural Marxists," have tried to identify a somewhat softer position than that advanced by the so-called "instrumental Marxists" (two very good sources are Greenberg, 1981 and Beirne and Quinney, 1982). Among other things, they see the state and its various agencies as sometimes being a more or less independent power rather than as little more than a "managing committee" for the bourgeoisie. Still, we find a good deal of merit in Thompson's (1982: 130-131) critical summary of the Marxist position on law:

> . . . it is clearly an instrument of the *de facto* ruling class: it both defines and defends these rulers' claims upon resources and labour-power—it says what shall be property and what shall be crime—and it mediates class relations with a set of appropriate rules and sanctions, all of which, ultimately, confirm and consolidate existing class power. Hence the rule of law is only another mask for the rule of a class.

In all fairness to past and present advocates of a class conflict theory of law—and they have done much to advance our understanding of how frequently law as well as the administration of law advances the position of the powerful to the detriment of others—they seem to fall victim to several attacks. First, more than a few of them are, on an ideological level, thoroughly convinced that there simply must be a ruling elite out there somewhere. Claims from others that evidence must be put on the top of the table to support such an assertion and to show how such a ruling elite actually uses law to protect or enhance its advantaged position are too often laughed at. Why should we or anyone else, Marxists argue, be asked to prove what is so clearly self-evident?

More sophisticated Marxists (that is, the structural rather than the instrumental Marxists) are themselves hostile toward so obviously silly a position. Recently, for example, Beirne and Quinney (1982: 17) suggest that instrumental Marxists and others who share their point of view

> must continually be embarrassed by empirical evidence. Dominant classes are typically unable to manipulate state apparatuses (which? when? where?) at will and despite all political opposition. Do legislative and judicial institutions have no degree of autonomy, no internal histories? Is all legislation, and are the activities of all personnel within the legal system, always to be explained by the convenient *deus ex màchina* of the interests of dominant classes?

Secondly, some if not most Marxists have a really aggravating way of seeming to suggest that everyday, ordinary citizens have an IQ roughly equal to that of a post. We see little to support such an attitude. Instead, we find more of merit in a portion of E. P. Thompson's critique of the Marxist position that goes like this (1982: 133):

> people are not as stupid as some structuralist philosophers suppose them to be . . . Most men have a strong sense of justice, at least with regard to their own interests. If the law is evidently partial and unjust, then it will mask nothing, legitimize nothing, contribute nothing to any class's hegemony. The essential precondition for the effectiveness of law, in its function as ideology, is that it shall display an independence from gross manipulation and shall seem to be just. It cannot seem to be so without upholding its own logic and criteria of equity; indeed, on occasion, by actually being just . . . it is not often the case that a ruling ideology can be dismissed as a mere hypocrisy; even rulers find a need to legitimize their power, to moralize their functions, to feel themselves to be useful and just . . . The law may be rhetoric, but it need not be empty rhetoric.

Finally, and here we are thinking largely in terms of the structural Marxists, the contemporary inclination to allow for a good deal of "give and take" in the law-making, law-modifying, and law-applying processes, and also the willingness to grant significant degrees of autonomy to the state and its various administrative components, seems to give rise to an awfully "fuzzy" species of Marxism. Taken to something of an extreme, this brand of Marxism is not at all different from the position advanced by the intergroup conflict perspective to which we will be turning our attention in a moment. Even if not taken to an extreme, the only apparent differences between some structural Marxists and some intergroup conflict theorists are twofold.

First, the former group is inclined to think in terms of fairly crisp and clean *class* distinctions that are created by differences in the relationships that exist between various categories of the population (for example, the bourgeoisie, the proletariat, and so on) and the means of production. The latter group is far more inclined to speak in terms of variations in *socioeconomic status*, which is both a more ambiguous concept and one that is far less determined by the means of production one might find at any given point in time.

Second, the former group tends to include persons with more of a zeal for bringing about fundamental changes in the nature of our social, economic, and political arrangements (i.e., the notion of *praxis*). The latter group is at least somewhat more inclined to think of their work as being a scholarly product that has inherent value even if it is not used by them or by others as an instrument by means of which social change is brought about.

The Interest Group Conflict Model

We will make no matter-of-fact claim that law is or must be the product of any particular set of forces. Neither will we contend that the forces that give rise to a particular law (or a particular way of applying a given law) are the same forces that lead us to retain that law (or pattern of applying that law) over time. What can be said without fear of contradiction is that all law, because it is a set of formal rules whose violation carries with it some likelihood of intervention by the state, is an expression of interests. It does not flow from some set of immutable truths, for no such absolute truths have been revealed to us during the long course of human history. It may or may not have some broad and preexisting support in the customs, values, and moral standards of a people either with regard to its broad outlines or its specific provisions. It may or may not reveal or perpetuate some deep schism between the advantaged and the disadvantaged segments of our population. What law and its application do reveal is the successful use of power at a given point in time by one or more sets of actors. The same is true, of course, with regard to those areas—and they are many—to which the provisions of public and or private law do not reach. Dominant interests may sometimes be served just as effectively by the absence as by the availability of law.

Law, in short, may perhaps best be characterized as both an independent and a dependent variable, as a set of formal rules that is at once the product of interests and a powerful means by which interests are protected and enhanced (see, for example, Akers and Hawkins, 1975; Beirne and Quinney, 1982; Kairys, 1982; Chambliss and Seidman,

1982; and Thomas and Hepburn, 1983). Regarding any specific legal prohibition or requirement (or, of course, the absence of any legal prohibition or requirement), one will surely find more or less consensus, more or less of an exercise of economic power, and more or less of a conscious or nonconscious effort on the part of the media to mobilize interests (see, for instance, Hagan, 1980). One might hypothesize, for example, that elements of consensus will be easier to identify in the case of *mala in se* offenses and less easy to identify in the case of *mala prohibita* offenses. Similarly, one might well expect to find a more obvious manifestation of economic interests in such noncriminal areas of law as patent law, copyright law, contract law, tort law, and a host of other areas of law that might serve those interests well.

But the "bottom line," most particularly within the context of a complex society such as ours, is that law will appear (or disappear) and be applied (or ignored) in a manner that reflects a victory—even if only a purely symbolic victory—for one set of interests at the expense, virtually by definition, of competing interests. Stated somewhat differently as we prepare to examine alternative justifications for the punishment provisions that are attached to criminal laws, law is not properly to be thought of as a neutral set of rules the legitimacy of which is somehow to be taken for granted. True, when those very special kinds of rules are applied to specific actors who are said to have violated them, it is our moral obligation to punish only in some fashion for which we can advance what is to us a firm justification. But to consume ourselves with the problems of who is to be punished and how we are to determine the amount of deserved punishment without having first concerned ourselves with how and why some bit of conduct came to be defined as a violation of criminal law would be to attribute more legitimacy and more moral value to the status quo of criminal law than criminal law deserves.

JUSTIFYING PUNISHMENT:
PROBLEMS IN MORAL PHILOSOPHY

In the previous section of this chapter we have tried to show that the legitimacy of the content of law is something that must never be taken for granted and that it is instead a fundamental problem for those interested in any type of public or private law. Now, however, we need to simplify what follows by stipulating in advance (1) that we have narrowed the focus of our attention to the provisions of substantive criminal law and (2) that we have somehow established to the satisfaction of all concerned that we are dealing with a body of criminal law that is uniformly worthy of our respect.

In this Candide-like best of all possible worlds we quickly come upon a problem that is at once as complex and as critically important as any one can find in any legal system. It is the problem of punishment, with the term punishment in this formal context being defined as any "lawfully imposed pain, suffering, or loss of otherwise available rights imposed on a culpable actor as a consequence of unlawful action or inaction" (Thomas and Hepburn, 1983: 544). At a minimum, any reasonable effort to resolve the various problems associated with punishment must address the following concerns. First, what is the rationale for attaching punishment provisions to that set of rules we refer to as our body of criminal law? Second, on whom may punishment justly be imposed? Third, what objective(s) do we seek to achieve by punishing those who are deemed to be eligible for punishment? (And here you should carefully note the need to distinguish between efforts to justify a system of rules—that is, criminal laws—which provides for punishment and the actual imposition of punishment on particular actors who are believed to have violated those rules.) Finally, on what basis are we to determine the amount or type of punishment that a blameworthy actor should receive?

If there is anything in the fields of criminology and criminal law that one may take as a self-evident truth, then surely it is this: The maturity and the quality of a civilized society is directly proportional to the moral gravity it attaches to the imposition of punishment on any of its members. When the lives and liberties of any or of all citizens within a society are treated in a cavalier fashion, then it necessarily follows that the moral stature of the entire society is in some measure diminished. From this axiom one may derive a corollary that is of special relevance to the present discussion: A quick but meaningful litmus test of the moral fiber of any society flows from an assessment of how that society protects the lives and liberties of its most marginal members. Marginality in this context refers to those who occupy the least advantaged social positions—perhaps in contemporary American society those who are poor, the objects of racial or religious discrimination, females, advocates of especially unpopular political positions, and various others—and those who by their actions or inactions have violated basic social expectations—a group that surely includes many if not most of those who violate the provisions of criminal law, but also, for instance, those who are said to be mentally ill.

In a relative if not, unfortunately, in an absolute sense, those in this society should derive some satisfaction from our social and legal attentiveness to those who, depending upon your political ideology and the specific facts being scrutinized, either have moved or been driven toward the margins of our social system. Perhaps especially in the area of criminal law and its administration, a host of substantive and procedural constraints stand between the awesome power of the state and its desire to impose punishment. Obvious examples of these limitations will be described in this as well as other portions of our discussion of substantive criminal law. Many others—as with limitations on how the state may go about the business of obtaining evidence to support criminal prosecutions, First Amendment protections regarding the free exercise of speech, religion, and assembly, the Sixth Amendment guarantee of right to counsel and trial by jury, and the Eighth Amendment protections against excessive bail and the imposition of cruel and unusual punishments—are now fairly firmly established. In addition, for hundreds of years philosophers, legal scholars, and many others have spilled gallons of ink on thousands of pages in their quest for a viable set of answers to the questions we posed earlier. Why do we have criminal law? Who is eligible for punishment? How do we determine the punishment that is deserved? What is it that we seek to achieve when we permit punishment to be imposed?

The answers to these questions are legion and, in truth, those answers leave much to be desired (for some fairly readable reviews see Pincoffs, 1966; Hart, 1968; Gerber and McAnany, 1972; Feinberg and Gross, 1975; Bedau, 1978; Fletcher, 1978; Gross, 1979; Gross and von Hirsch, 1981; and Murphy, 1985). Further, the few pages that we can devote to these questions can be relied on as nothing more than a sketchy introduction to an exceedingly large and often complex literature. Keeping this important caveat in mind, we will attempt to put forward the basic positions advanced by each of three major groups: the retributivists, the utilitarians, and, for want of a better term, the rehabilitationists.

Retributivism as a Justification for Punishment

Although there are any number of variations on the retributivist theme, it is at its core a "backward-looking" perspective whose proponents commonly contend that we have a moral obligation to impose a type or degree of punishment on blameworthy offenders consistent with the harmfulness of their unlawful conduct (see, for instance, Hart, 1968; Bedau, 1978). Retributivists have an image of human behavior that depicts actors as having the ability to choose on a purely rational basis between good and evil, noncriminal and criminal alternatives. Should they voluntarily select the criminal option, then it is morally just that they be punished. Quite importantly, they deserve to be punished because of the harmfulness of their blameworthy conduct and not as a consequence of any hope that their punishment might serve such future benefits as crime prevention. Instead, it is asserted that "the return of suffering for moral evil voluntarily done is itself just or morally good" (Bedau, 1978: 602-603). Furthermore, the amount or type of punishment which may be justified is limited by what is referred to as the *principle of just deserts* or the *principle of proportionality.* The contention is that no offender may justly receive any greater—or any lesser—punishment than that dictated by the harmfulness of his or her conduct.

In many ways, of course, this preliminary statement of the retributivist position ignores at least two very important problems. To begin with, few of us would think of criminal law as being a special set of rules we created purely to legitimate and justify our right to punish and with no other objective in mind. Secondly, to contend that the guilty should be punished in accordance with some notion of proportionality may provide a point of departure for those wishing to create a just system of punishment. It provides them with nothing, however, regarding the specific punishments that would be equal to some notion of just dessert. Each of these problems requires some additional comment.

Little needs to be said regarding whether retributivists must ignore altogether the future consequences of punishment. It is sufficient to note our agreement with Hart (1968) and others who draw distinctions between the general purposes of our system of criminal law and the various justifications that have been put forward regarding the particular objectives of the punishment provisions that may be incorporated into that body of law. All systems of criminal law reflect an interest in the attainment of fairly obvious goals. They seek to increase the likelihood of desired forms of behavior and to decrease the likelihood of undesired conduct. Thus, even the "backward-looking" character of a retributivist position has some initial "forward-looking" elements.

The distribution of punishments made available within our body of criminal law is a good deal more problematic. All that has been made clear thus far is that only blameworthy actors (that is, those found guilty of voluntary criminal acts) are eligible to be punished. To know *who* is eligible and *when* eligibility exists tells us nothing about how *much* beyond some awfully vague notions of the type represented by the principle of just dessert or proportionality. Here, unfortunately, is where retributivists begin to move toward a swamp from which they seem entirely unable to escape. Their efforts to do so, however, generally take one of two or perhaps three basic forms (Hart, 1968; Feinberg and Gross; 1975; Morris, 1982).

The first of these forms contains the implication that for each and every morally blameworthy act there is some particular type or degree of punishment that is deserved. This form is often said to view a retributive theory as a source for *defining principles of punishment*. This position, in turn, can be divided in two ways. One of these, perhaps as initially reflected in *lex talionis* provisions of the Code of Hammurabi more than 3,000 years ago, suggests that "the punishment should match the crime not only in the degree of harm inflicted on its victim, but also in the mode and manner of infliction: fines for larceny, physical beatings for battery, capital punishment for death" (Feinberg and Gross, 1975: 4). For instance, in the Code of Hammurabi one finds such provisions as "If a man has struck his father, his hands one shall cut off" and "If a man has made the tooth of a man that is his equal to fall out, one shall make his tooth fall out. Relatively few elements of this *in-kind retributivism* exist in modern systems of criminal law. However, an alternative application of retributivism as a defining principle is often encountered in various criminal laws that require the imposition of a highly specific sentence on all persons who have committed a particular offense.

A rather different variation on this retributive theme depicts retributive notions of just dessert as a source of *limiting principles of punishment*. Such a position would presumably define for us "the outer limits of leniency and severity which should not be exceeded" (Morris, 1982: 183). One commonly finds such a notion reflected in modern bodies of criminal law. For example, Florida law (chapter 775.082 of the Florida Criminal Code) demands that any person convicted of a capital felony who does not receive a sentence of death "shall be punished by life imprisonment and shall be required to serve no less than 25 years before becoming eligible for parole." (Here we should emphasize that those factors that might be employed to reduce the punishment of an offender from life imprisonment to some less harsh actual sentence commonly involve influences—responsiveness to rehabilitative efforts, degree of prison overcrowding, and so on—that few if any retributivists would define as being morally defensible.)

The appeal of some features of the retributive position is quite obvious. True, many if not most of us have a worldview that places a premium on the future benefits of our actions, policies, laws, and so on. Our adherence to the notion that punishing criminals is an important way of "teaching them a lesson" and thereby preventing future harmful conduct illustrates this point quite well. Retributivists stoutly deny that punishing persons in order to achieve these or other future benefits has a moral justification. On the other hand, we have a fondness for such notions as "balancing the scales of justice" and "paying debts to society."

The same is true regarding the vague feeling that those who do not "play by the rules" are somehow taking advantage of those who choose more conventional behavioral options. These ideas, of course, are at the very core of the retributive theory of punishment.

Before you leap at the opportunity to describe yourself as a retributivist, take a moment or two to frame answers for two rather sharp thorns that retributivists often find lodged in a portion of their anatomy that makes resting on their principles a bit uncomfortable. First, regardless of whether retributive theories are thought of as a source of either defining or of limiting principles of punishment, where, in effect, does a faithful retributivist find his or her precise sentencing scheme?

Assume, for instance, that you have been employed as the retributive philosopher to whom a sentencing judge will be required to turn for advice prior to his or her imposing a sentence on a properly convicted offender. The first offender to attract your mutual interest proves to be an unemployed, largely uneducated Hispanic young man who has been remarkably unsuccessful in providing a reasonable quality of life for his wife and three children. The young man freely admits that he committed an act of unarmed robbery and, indeed, that he documents precisely how he and his family used all of the proceeds he obtained from his crime. At his sentencing hearing he even admits quite freely to a prior conviction for shoplifting. The sentencing judge turns to you with a request that you, free from all constraints of criminal law, select either a particular punishment (for example, five years in the state penitentiary) or a particular range of punishment (for instance, four to six years in the same penitentiary). What is your response? Where, as a matter of "pure" retributive principle, did you find the "just" sentence? Furthermore, did you (or should you) base your decision on your assessment of the young man's economic status, his family obligations, and/or his prior criminal record?

The point of this exercise, of course, is to convince you that there are no fixed or correct retributive answers to these very troublesome questions. Indeed, it is true that two equally committed retributivists could approach this very same set of facts and, with an equal likelihood of their being entirely steadfast in their commitment to fundamental retributive principles, arrive at vastly different solutions to the sentencing problem we have created.

Second, does a commitment to retributivism flatly demand that the blameworthy offender be punished in accordance with some unfortunately vague notion of just dessert? Or, alternatively, does it simply permit the blameworthy to be punished while holding out the possibility that punishment would be avoided as a consequence of some other consideration? What if any role, for example, is to be played by such concepts as mercy or forgiveness? Must they be brushed aside as though they either did not exist or were irrelevant to the problems before us? And what of other considerations? What, for instance, if it could be established to the satisfaction of all concerned that, on the one hand, a deserved punishment was so harsh that it was certain to later drive the alienated offender to further crime or, on the other hand, that a deserved punishment was so lenient that it would erode away the aversion that others might have toward the conduct being punished? We see little in the stance commonly taken by retributivists that yields meaningful answers to such questions as these (but see, for example, Morris, 1982: 179-209).

Utilitarianism and the Criminal Sanction

We have devoted a good deal of attention to retribution as a theory that seeks to justify punishment largely because of contemporary interest in such retributive or quasiretributive approaches as those that involve sentencing guidelines, "fixed" or presumptive sentences, the abolition of parole, and various other strategies whose aim is—or at least claims to be—giving offenders their just desserts. Now, however, we will have to be quite brief in our treatment of utilitarian and rehabilitative models. First, with regard to the utilitarian model, we encounter something of a counterpoint to retributive contentions. Although the utilitarians share the retributivists image of humans who are endowed with the inherent ability to freely choose between good and evil alternatives, and although there is certainly an agreement among utilitarians that the general purpose of criminal law is preventative, there is sharp disagreement on virtually all other matters.

To begin with, utilitarian theories of punishment are fundamentally "forward looking" rather than "backward-looking." Punishment is depicted as being altogether without a moral foundation unless it can be shown to achieve one or more future benefits. Those future benefits, all of which fall within the general scope of crime prevention, are at least three in number: *general deterrence, specific deterrence*, and *incapacitation*. General deterrence refers to how the threat or actual imposition of punishment elevates the risk perceptions of persons other than those who are the objects of punishment. Specific deterrence refers to how the actual imposition of punishment shapes the subsequent risk perceptions of those who are the objects of punishment. Incapacitation refers to the ability of punishment to limit or eliminate altogether the opportunities offenders would otherwise have to violate the law.

The basic deterrence thesis is that we are all rational creatures who, because we are primarily motivated by our narrow self-interests, will select those courses of action from which we expect (rightly or wrongly) to derive the greatest number of benefits or rewards at the lowest cost. Thus, the hypothesis is that people will refrain from engaging in crime if the threat of punishment convinces them that criminal conduct is not in their self-interest. Incapacitation is quite a different notion. There, no special importance is attached to whether punishment does or does not elevate our perception of the costs of criminal choices. Instead, the focus is on the availability of criminal opportunities and on how one or more types of punishment might prevent crime simply by reducing access to such opportunities. Were we to place those who steal automobiles in prison for some period of time, for example, does it really matter that they may not have been "taught the lesson" that "crime doesn't pay"? The answer, of course, is that it matters not whether they perceive stealing cars to carry unacceptable risks of punishment—at least for the duration of their prison terms. So long as our hypothetical offender remains incarcerated in an institution within which no cars are to be found, then our offender will steal no cars. The opportunity to do so does not exist even if the willingness to accept the risk persists.

The utilitarians' objective, in short, is to impose the punishment that is sufficient to serve the general goal of crime prevention. Thus, in Jeremy Bentham's influential work, *Introduction to Principles of Morals and Legislation*, we find the assertion that "[T]he general object which all laws have, or ought to have, in common, is to augment the total happiness of the community; and therefore ... to exclude, as far as may be, everything that tends to subtract from that happiness." (Bentham, 1975: 25). Further, punishment, seen by virtually all as an immoral and evil act unless it is imposed in accordance with sound justifications, is depicted as being inappropriate unless it serves some useful purpose. "Upon the principle of utility, if it ought at all to be admitted, it ought only to be admitted in as far as it promises to exclude some greater evil" (Bentham, 1975: 25). This promise, say the utilitarians, is most likely to be fulfilled when punishment has the attributes of *swiftness, certainty,* and adequate *severity.* In this context, swiftness refers to the time lag between law violations and reactions to those violations, certainty to the likelihood that violations will elicit some reactions, and severity, of course, to the amount of punishment that is imposed. It is quite important, however, that deficiencies in one or more of these three areas are said to be correctable if the opportunity to manipulate the value of other areas exists. To again rely upon Bentham (1975: 30, emphasis in the original), it is asserted that "*Want of certainty must be made up in magnitude*" and that "*Punishment must be further increased in point of magnitude, in proportion as it falls short in point of proximity.*"

Not unlike the retributivist position described previously, there is much in the contrary utilitarian viewpoint that has an appeal to most if not to all of us. Here, too, however, there are a host of problems that cannot be escaped cleanly. First of all, the image of all criminal and noncriminal acts being the product of some advanced and careful balancing of perceived costs and rewards, risks and benefits simply does not ring true when it is compared with our present knowledge about human behavior. Risk calculation is a variable, not a constant. Sometimes it is quite obviously present. However, as is the case with many serious crimes committed against persons, the behavior is often quite spontaneous (see, for instance, Thomas and Hepburn, 1983: 124-136; 226-236).

Second, especially with regard to specific deterrence and incapacitation hypotheses, there is much contradictory evidence regarding the future benefits of punishment. For example, in some of our own recent research (Thomas and Bishop, 1985) we found that those who reported encounters with the criminal justice system had lower perceptions of the risks associated with unlawful conduct than was true of those who had no such contacts. Experiencing processing within the juvenile and criminal justice systems often teaches those having the experience that the risk of punishment is far lower than they once may have imagined. Similarly, the incapacitative effects of punishment often are overestimated. With regard to many profit-motivated forms of criminal behavior, for instance, it seems clear that the potential rewards of crime tend to increase when the risks associated with that criminal conduct increase. Many drug offenses serve as an obvious illustration of this reality. Drug distributors are apprehended and punished. This may elevate relevant perceptions of risk, but it also tends to increase the cost—and therefore the potential rewards associated with—the prohibited conduct. At some point it is more than possible that the growing potential for quick rewards reaches a point at which persons previously fearful of punishment are drawn into the very type of behavior that the application of punishment sought to prevent.

Finally, much as the utilitarians have to say about how we can justify our body of criminal law, who they are willing to define as being eligible for punishment, and what they take to be the proper goals of punishment, they have remarkably little to offer regarding the amount of punishment that may justly be imposed. To say that the punishment must be no more and no less than what is required to achieve future benefits certainly distinguishes the utilitarians from the retributivists. However, the position is totally lacking when one attempts to derive from it tangible sentencing guidelines. Especially when the views of the utilitarians have been translated into legal policy, the results often have been harsh to the extreme. Legislative bodies enact a new criminal law with the general objective of preventing some type of presumably harmful behavior. Punishment is imposed on those who violate the law. The behavior persists. The law is modified to provide for harsher punishment. The behavior still persists. Punishment is enhanced once again. Yet those making our criminal law remain unshaken in their conviction that sooner or later they will find a punishment that surely will be so harsh that no rational person will accept the risk of confronting it. In theory, to be sure, such draconian legislative efforts would find no support. Were any punishment to have the "on balance" effect of causing more mischief and unhappiness than it prevented, then it would be devoid of any moral justification. Here, however, lofty theory and the tangible provisions of criminal law are often quite detached from one another.

Rehabilitation as a Goal of Sentencing

We must begin our consideration of rehabilitative theories as a means of justifying the sentences imposed by our criminal courts with a good deal of care. There are at least two important reasons for our caution.

First of all, rehabilitative theories are fundamentally different from both retributive and utilitarian theories in terms of their image of the basic causes of criminal behavior. Although retributivists and utilitarians disagree with one another about many aspects of punishment, they are alike in their view that punishment is only justifiable when offenders exercise their freedom of choice and choose criminal rather than noncriminal courses of action. Were either group of theorists to encounter persons who could not be defined as morally responsible actors whose voluntary actions caused harm, then neither would accept punishment as a morally sound societal response. In stark contrast to this point of view, rehabilitative theorists contend that criminal behavior is the consequence of influences over which individual offenders lack any meaningful degree of control. Instead, offenders are depicted as persons who either are drawn to or driven to crime by forces other than free choice. The specific causal influences to which rehabilitative theorists point are quite diverse. For example, some identify biological influences, some point to psychological forces, some emphasize social psychological factors, and still others point to such more general variables as sexism, racism, economic inequality, and political oppression. These pronounced differences between rehabilitative theories notwithstanding, all emphasize one basic proposition: *Criminal behavior, rather than reflecting harmful conduct freely by rational actors who deserve to be held responsible for the harm they willingly caused, is little more than a consequence of forces over which they lack control and for which they have no responsibility.*

Second, this image of crime as something either precisely the same as, or remarkably similar to, little more than a symptom of some underlying disease drives rehabilitative theorists to take a very negative stance on the appropriateness of punishment (see, for instance, Menninger, 1968; Conrad and Schneider, 1980; Cullen and Gilbert, 1982). Punishment, they contend, is a reaction that may be appropriate if we encounter persons who freely chose to violate the law, but it is without justification in all cases in which crime is more properly viewed as the behavior of something other than rationale choice. It would be far more appropriate, they argue, for us to avoid terms like "punishment" altogether and, instead, to view the sentencing of convicted offenders as nothing more or less than an opportunity for the state to intervene in the lives of such persons with the sole objective of attacking the underlying causes of the criminal behavior. In other words, the objective of sentencing should be to intervene with the objective of treating the offender rather than to punish with the objective either of giving the offender his or her just deserts (that is, following a retributive theory) or of seeking to prevent crime through such mechanisms as deterrence and incapacitation (in other words, following a utilitarian theory).

At first glance the position of the rehabilitative theorists has a certain attractiveness. For example, it seems benevolent rather than punitive. Especially when rehabilitative theorists inject heavy doses of biological, medical, or psychiatric jargon, their approach also appeals to our excessive fondness for consigning various types of difficult jobs to appropriate groups of experts whose specialized training has provided them with more expertise than the vast majority of us have to offer. Finally, few of us would support the punishment of persons who were not responsible for their conduct even if the consequences of that conduct were quite harmful. Indeed, as we will see when we reach chapter 6, our system of criminal law has accepted a host of excuses or justifications as legal defenses for hundreds of years. The foundation for many of those defenses is that the person charged with an offense should not be held criminally liable because his or her behavior was not the outcome of a morally responsible actor freely and voluntarily choosing to violate the law.

Unfortunately, the rehabilitative model has proven to be like various other glittering objects that prove to be something far less valuable than gold. The problems it presents can be categorized in a variety of ways, but here we will deal briefly with only its conceptual, political, and practical defects.

First of all, the rehabilitative model is flawed on a conceptual level because it urges us to accept—and to accept on the basis of pitifully little factual evidence—the thesis that crime is essentially a disease entity that calls for treatment rather than punishment. At its worst, such a contention is simple minded. Even at its best, the contention greatly exaggerates the notion of determinism that is at the core of all contemporary behavior science theories of crime. The simple-minded version typically relies on the following circular logic (or illogic). Presupposing that crime is some sort of disease, we are asked to determine whether a particular actor is or is not "sick" and therefore in need of treatment. The determination is made by asking whether or not the actor has violated the law. If he or she has violated the law, then he or she is judged to be "sick," to be in need of treatment. Such a classification is totally absurd. It cannot be proven to be false—and it also cannot be proven to be correct. It could only become useful were the illness hypothesis capable of being supported by evidence other than that provided by proof of guilt or innocence, and in the vast majority of cases no such evidence exists.

Even an avoidance of the simple-minded versions of the rehabilitative model does not permit us to go much further. For example, to say that crime can be caused by such factors as low levels of educational attainment, insufficiently developed vocational skills, blocked access to opportunities in the conventional world, poverty, racism, and dozens of other influences cannot be taken to mean that persons confronting such criminogenic influences have no control over their behavior and consequently no responsibility for the harm their behavior may cause. The vast majority of those who confront all of these problems on a routine basis commonly refrain from engaging in criminal conduct. If such problems are truly as powerful as some contend, then why is it that the rates of crime among them are not massively higher? Surely part of the reason is that human beings are not pushed and pulled in their everyday lives in a fashion that is like that of ping-pong balls being batted from one side of a table to another. They can and do make choices—although the circumstances they confront quite obviously can either increase or decrease the range of the options to which they have access.

Beyond such conceptual problems as these are some tediously complex political concerns. However, it is fair and reasonable to argue that the rehabilitative model, at least as that model has been implemented in the routine operation of our juvenile and criminal justice systems, is inherently conservative if it is evaluated in purely political terms. The reasons why this is true are legion. Advocates of the model have accepted the reasonableness and legitimacy of our body of criminal law without raising meaningful questions about whose interests are served (or oppressed) by that body of law. They have accepted with few questions or complaints the validity of decisions made within a criminal justice system whose decision-making processes too often produce outcomes that are characterized by unfairness, arbitrariness, and discrimination. Finally, by focusing our attention on characteristics of individual offenders as the root causes of crime and delinquency, virtually all applications of the rehabilitative model draw our attention away from the defects and deficiencies we find in the basic structure of social arrangements that routinely give rise to elevated rates of criminal behavior. How humane and benevolent is it, for example, if we seek to treat individual offenders with surgery, drugs, individual or group psychotherapy, or a host of other strategies while we leave largely untouched the structure of a society that deprives huge portions of its population from meaningful access to social, economic, and political power? One suspects that it is roughly as useful as is our inclination to place a free turkey on the table of an impoverished family on Thanksgiving or Christmas and to walk away from our well-motivated degradation of that family with the pious conviction that we just struck a major blow in the fight against poverty.

Finally, the rehabilitative model is flawed on a purely practical level. For almost a full century a growing number of our criminal codes and penal practices sought to attribute significance to the notion that offenders should be treated and rehabilitated rather than punished. The effort has involved tens of thousands of "expert correctional practitioners," hundreds of thousands of convicted offenders, and billions of dollars of expenditures. The rate of crime in the larger society has been affected not at all. Time after time, efforts to measure the impact of treatment efforts on the objects of those efforts have failed to show that those efforts were beneficial (see, for instance, Bailey, 1966; Kassenbaum et al., 1971; Morris, 1974; Lerman, 1975; Lipton et al., 1975; Riedel and Thornberry, 1978; Thomas, 1986). What we do find is hundreds of thousands of offenders confronting massive deprivations of liberty for protracted periods of time with those deprivations being justified as a necessary condition for their effective treatment. But the promised treatment seldom produced the predicted results. It is ironic. Were 100 years of experience to reveal that the claimed benefits of harsh and intrusive methods of treating our dogs and cats to yield similarly few real benefits, veterinarians all over the country would be starving to death. When precisely the same negative record is established by correctional experts, we ask whether they have been given enough time, enough power, and enough resources. If there is real sickness to be found, one is led to wonder whether it is a problem of the keepers as opposed to one of the kept.

SUMMARY

The objective of this chapter has been twofold. First, it provided us with an opportunity to examine contrary perspectives on the origins or sources of law. Our examination of natural law, consensus, interest group conflict, and class conflict theories revealed a good deal of disagreement about the origins and uses of law. None of these theories proved to be an entirely adequate explanation. Part of this insufficiency, however, must be attributed to important differences one encounters as one moves from one type of law to another and other differences that are associated with the type of analysis upon which one relies. The origins of some criminal laws, for example, do appear to have a firm foundation in the basic sentiments, values, and moral standards of the culture within which they are found. This is perhaps best illustrated by the aversion that virtually all have to such offenses as murder, rape, assault, and many theft offenses. The same cannot be said about a large number of other laws (for example, tax laws, draft registration statutes, laws that seek to prohibit such "victimless crimes" as gambling, many forms of drug use, abortion, homosexuality, and so on). At the same time, however, when we examine the specific provisions of laws—even of those laws that seek to prohibit forms of behavior that almost all of us view as properly falling within the realm of criminal law—consensus commonly gives way to clashing interests of competing groups and sometimes to fairly obvious conflicts between classes of people who are separate from one another by their vastly differing social and economic positions.

Attention also was given to contrary perspectives on how we can or should justify the punishment provisions of criminal law. We found that the retributive, utilitarian, and rehabilitative models share only a single common denominator. Each sees one or more facets of our body of criminal law as a means of increasing the likelihood of desired forms of conduct and decreasing the incidence of undesired conduct. On most other dimensions those who advocate these models are in sharp disagreement with one another regarding how to best justify punishment—or, in the case of those favoring the rehabilitative model, how to best justify the nonpunitive intervention of the state. As proven to be true regarding theories of the origins of law, these theories of the proper purposes of punishment (or of intervention) proved to have significant conceptual and practical limitations. Perhaps this is why so many of our penal practices are defended by claims that they are partly retributive, partly utilitarian, and partly rehabilitative. It should now be obvious, however, that any effort to blend these three models together in any reasonable or logical way is all but totally impossible.

Now, however, the time has come for us to move away from alternative theories of the origins of law and competing justifications for punishment and toward a systematic consideration of important principles of substantive criminal law. We will begin that significant portion of our study of law by considering some basic constitutional limitations that have been placed on what may and what may not be properly defined as a crime within our system of criminal jurisprudence.

DISCUSSION QUESTIONS

1. Given the fundamental democratic principles that we claim to support in our political system, to what extent should provisions of law reflect the special interests of some groups or classes of persons? To what extent do provisions of criminal (and also our civil) law reflect such interests?

2. Assume that Joe caused much financial harm to the owner of a small store in his quest to escape from the impoverished plight he and his family confronted. Assume, for instance, that he broke into the store late one evening and stole $10,000 worth of property. What variables should be taken into account, and what specific sentence (if any) should be imposed on Joe within a system of justice committed entirely to a retributive theory of punishment? What would change if the system were committed entirely to utilitarian principles? To rehabilitative principles?

4

CONSTITUTIONAL LIMITS ON CRIMINAL LAW

It should now be obvious that there are vast disparities in how one can approach the very difficult task of providing an acceptable moral justification for the hypothetical right of the state to impose punishment on its citizens. Each point of view, however, seeks to create an image of the proper scope of criminal law. Each approaches the task of setting such limits primarily by attempting to define who shall be deemed eligible for punishment, the type or degree of punishment that offenders either may or must receive, and the goal(s) that punishment must serve if it is to meet minimum moral standards.

These aspects of moral and legal philosophy aside, we need to delve more deeply into our study of the purposes and limitations of criminal law. Within the particular context of our system of criminal law, we need to identify the set of specific limitations that actually have been placed on efforts to make or to apply the provisions of criminal law. This does not mean that fundamental principles of moral and legal philosophy are now to be ignored altogether. It does mean that we will drift away from notions regarding what limitations *ought to be* placed on criminal law to a somewhat more practical assessment of the limitations that *are* placed on it.

We should admit from the beginning that identifying a reasonable method of organizing this portion of the discussion has presented us with a difficult task. Our preference would be to ignore matters pertaining to criminal procedure and to limit our focus to topics that fall within the scope of substantive criminal law. Unfortunately, basic legal limitations on the scope of criminal law simply cannot be so cleanly divided into procedural and substantive law categories. This fact will soon become quite obvious. An alternative approach requires identifying those limits we now place on the scope or reach of criminal law that are set forth in or derived from basic constitutional principles. To pursue that approach we will turn our attention first to those limitations that originate in the language of the Constitution itself and then to those that flow from the Bill of Rights and the due process clause of the Fourteenth Amendment.

LIMITATIONS SET FORTH IN THE CONSTITUTION

prohibited

Bills of Attainder and Bills of Punishment

The federal Constitution, which was ratified in 1789, is essentially a document, the authors of which sought to describe the relationship that was to exist between the states and the federal government and the rights and duties of various elected and appointed officers of the federal government. Put more simply, the Constitution is not a document in which we find much that is of specific relevance to those concerned with either substantive criminal law or criminal procedure. There are, however, at least two noteworthy exceptions to this general rule. Both may be found in Article I, Sections 9 and 10 of the Constitution. Specifically, Article I, Section 9(3) prohibits the Congress of the United States from enacting any Bill of Attainder or *ex post facto* law and Article I, Section 10(1) imposes an identical prohibition on the legislative bodies of the individual states.

The first of these limitations may be reviewed quite concisely. As a matter of early English common law a person who confessed to a felony, who was found guilty of a felony, or who was declared to be a felon after he or she escaped prosecution automatically lost a variety of civil and property rights. By the time of the American Revolution the common law notion of attainder had been transformed into actions taken by the English parliament. These actions came in one of two forms: *bills of attainder* and *bills of pains and punishment*. Bills of attainder took the form of a legislative decision to inflict sentences of death on specific persons believed to be guilty of serious felonies or acts of treason. Bills of pains and punishment took substantially the same form, but they involved the imposition of punishments other than death.

During and following the time of the Revolution the legislative bodies of all 13 colonies had adopted this practice of the English parliament (see, for instance, McNamara, 1982: 6). Very quickly, however, it was recognized that such practices were an open invitation to political oppression and that there was a clear need for "a general provision against arbitrary and tyrannical legislation over existing rights . . . " (*Ogden v. Saunders*, 25 U.S. [12 Wheat] 286 [1827]). Indeed, early in our constitutional history Supreme Court Justice Chase reflected back on these types of laws and observed that, "With very few exceptions, the advocates of such laws were stimulated by ambition, or personal resentment, and vindictive malice" (*Calder v. Bull*, 3 U.S. [3 Dall.] 386 [1798]). The firm conviction was that the power of the legislative branch to create law and the power of the judicial branch to impose punishment on those convicted of unlawful conduct must be kept separate. Because bills of attainder and bills of pains and penalty so obviously put members of legislative bodies into the position of being both legislators and judges, a flat prohibition against these practices was incorporated into the body of the Constitution.

The Prohibition Against
Ex Post Facto Laws

The prohibition against *ex post facto* laws presents us with a somewhat more complex concern. Certainly a significant part of the motivation to prohibit the enactment of *ex post facto* criminal laws has to do with what is often referred to as the *notice doctrine* (that is, the idea that ordinary citizens have a right to be placed on notice regarding the nature of any required or prohibited conduct in advance of any effort by the state to punishment them for violations of criminal law). In addition, most if not all of us feel that behavior should not be thought of as a violation of any rule unless the rule was created prior to any effort to use that rule. This is the way many of us interpret the meaning of *ex post facto* laws. There is, however, a good deal more to this constitutional limitation on criminal law than may be immediately apparent.

First of all, early judicial interpretations of this portion of the Constitution made it abundantly clear that it involved more than a simple articulation of the notice doctrine. In *Calder v. Bull* we find especially clear language:

> I[Justice Chase in delivering the majority opinion of the United States Supreme Court] will state what laws I consider *ex post facto* laws, within the words and the intent of the prohibition. 1st. Every law that makes an action done before the passing of the law, and which was innocent when done, criminal . . . 2d. Every law that aggravates a crime, or makes it greater than it was, when committed. 3d. Every law that changes the punishment, and inflicts a greater punishment, than the law annexed to the crime, when committed. 4th. Every law that alters the legal rules of evidence, and receives less, or different testimony, than the law required at the time of the commission of the offence, in order to convict the offender. All these, and similar laws, are mainfestly unjust and oppressive.

In effect, then, the Constitution forbids those making criminal law *either* to criminalize the conduct of a person after that person has engaged in conduct that was noncriminal at the time of the behavior *or* to change the "rules of the game" in such a way as to elevate an offender's risk of conviction or punishment beyond the risk he or she confronted when an unlawful act took place.

Secondly, a careful reading of the Constitution would leave one with the clear impression that the *ex post facto* law prohibition effects only the legislative branch of government. It forbids it to apply retroactively the provisions of criminal law that it has the power to create. The prohibition, however, has been given a far broader interpretation. Recognizing that the provisions of both substantive criminal law and rules of criminal procedure may become either broader or narrower as a consequence of judicial interpretation as well as legislative enactments, the United States Supreme Court has held that the prohibition applies to the activities of both the legislative and judicial branches of government. Clear language, for instance, may be found in *Marks v. United States*, 430 U.S. 191 (1977):

> the notion that persons have a right to fair warning of that conduct which will give rise to criminal penalties . . . is fundamental to our concept of constitutional liberty. As such that right is protected against judicial action by the Due Process Clause of the Fifth Amendment.

LIMITATIONS IMPOSED
BY THE BILL OF RIGHTS

The Bill of Rights, 10 amendments that were appended to the Constitution when they were ratified in 1791 and made applicable to criminal proceedings within the individual states through judicial interpretations of the due process and equal protection clause of the Fourteenth Amendment, provide the basis for a much larger set of limitations on both substantive criminal law and criminal procedure. Here we will limit our attention to five such limitations: *substantive equal protection, the overbreadth doctrine, the void for vagueness doctrine, the prohibition against double jeopardy, and the prohibition against the imposition of cruel and unusual punishment.*

Substantive Equal Protection

A thorough consideration of substantive equal protection is well beyond the scope of this brief volume. Essentially, however, the principle has been derived from judicial interpretations of the provisions of the Fifth and Fourteenth Amendments to the Constitution. It reflects support for the notion that our body of law should be fair and reasonable in terms of the manner in which it is applied (that is, due process of law) and in terms of the outcomes it creates (in other words, substantive equal protection). Our limited concern here is with how a commitment to substantive equal protection principles can limit the range of actions and inactions that fall within the realm of substantive criminal law.

This narrow concern may be served by one or two illustrations of how a law can be invalidated because of equal protection considerations. In *Eisenstadt v. Baird*, 405 U.S. 438 (1972), for example, the Supreme Court heard a challenge to a Massachusetts law that defined the distribution of contraceptives to unmarried persons as a crime. In effect, the substance of the law defined distribution of contraceptives to one class of persons (those who were married) as lawful but defined the same conduct as unlawful when it involved another class of persons (those who were single). Finding no rational basis for such a distinction, the law was held to be unconstitutional. Similarly, in *Loving v. Virginia*, 388 U.S. 1 (1967), the Court struck down a Virginia statute that prohibited interracial marriages. When a law defines conduct as lawful or unlawful purely on the basis of the race of the persons whose conduct is being evaluated, then the law cannot be permitted to stand (see, for example, *McLaughlin v. Florida*, 379 U.S. 184 [1964]).

Readers should take care not to extend equal protection arguments too far (see, for instance, *Michael M. v. Superior Court*, 450 U.S. 464 [1981]). To be sure, the courts have not taken a positive view of laws that appear to discriminate on the basis of such variables as sex, race, ethnicity, and religious preference, but the basic rationale for such negative assessments is that the courts find it nearly impossible to see how any legitimate interest of the state might be served by such factors as these (see, for example, *Reed v. Reed*, 404 U.S. 71 [1971]). On the other hand, one routinely encounters provisions of law that might seem to discriminate against a clearly defined class of persons but that do so in a manner that is acceptable to the appellate courts. For example, state laws commonly prohibit the sale of various substances like alcohol and cigarettes to minors and to define the possession of such substances by minors as unlawful. Do such laws undermine the rights of minors to equal protection of law? No. Generally speaking, the state has an obligation to protect the health and welfare of its citizens, and it traditionally has enjoyed broad latitude in determining how it will discharge that obligation to its younger citizens.

The point, then, is that any appearance of a criminal law having been drafted in such a way as to undermine the rights of citizens to equal protection of law is likely to provide a basis for challenges to the constitutionality of that law. For such a law to "pass constitutional muster," the state must be able to demonstrate that the law serves a legitimate interest. And even then the story is far from over. If a given law appears constitutionally sound on its face, it still may be challenged successfully if it is routinely applied in a discriminatory fashion.

The Overbreadth and Void for Vagueness Doctrines

It is entirely possible for a legislative body to create a criminal law that subsequently runs afoul of *either* the overbreath *or* the void for vagueness doctrines. The two limitations on criminal law are separable both in theory and in practice. Most commonly, however, challenges to the constitutionality of a given criminal law involving one of these legal principles also will involve the other. Thus, we will consider them within a single subsection of the present discussion.

Let us begin with the notion that a criminal law may be constitutionally defective because it is overbroad in its construction. The basic principle may be stated concisely. A criminal law is said to be defective if it clearly prohibits constitutionally protected conduct or might well be applied in such a way as to result in the punishment of those who have engaged in protected conduct (for instance, *Zwickler v. Koota*, 389 U.S. 241 [1967] and *Grayned v. City of Rockford*, 408 U.S. 104 [1972]). Generally speaking, therefore, any criminal law that seeks to inhibit the free exercise of speech, press, religion, or right to assemble peaceably either will or should be declared invalid by our courts because of overbreadth.

Assume, for instance, that a criminal law sought to punish any person who uses the flag or any representation of the flag of the United States with the intent of such use being to reflect a lack of respect for the government and citizens of the United States. Subsequent to the enactment of this statute, Joe, a self-styled Marxist, announces his intent to show his disrespect for the United States by offering for sale a new brand of toilet paper on which a facsimile of the flag has been reproduced. Should the new law be applied to Joe? The answer, of course, is that it should not. Under the overbreadth doctrine, Joe's protected freedom of speech, including symbolic speech, cannot be undermined by a criminal law (see, for example, *Smith v. Goguen*, 415 U.S. 566 [1974]).

The related void for vagueness doctrine presents us with at least somewhat more difficult problems. As the "void for vagueness" language suggests, a fundamental requirement that must be met by any criminal law is that it cannot be written in such a way that it is "so vague that men of common intelligence must guess at its meaning and differ as to its application" (*Connally v. General Construction Company*, 269 U.S. 385 [1926]). Implicit in this objection to vague statutory constructions is also the notion that they violate the notice doctrine mentioned earlier. In *United States v. Harriss*, 347 U.S. 612 (1954), for instance, the Court observed that a statute runs afoul of the vagueness doctrine if it "fails to give a person of ordinary intelligence fair notice that his contemplated conduct is forbidden by the statute." In other words, if the language of a criminal law is excessively vague and ambiguous, then it follows that "men of common intelligence" or "ordinary intelligence" would not have been placed effectively on notice regarding the precise nature of required or prohibited conduct. An old but still relevant case should be sufficient to illustrate the general aversion to vague statutes. In *Lanzetta v. New Jersey*, 306 U.S. 451 (1939) it was contended that the inclusion of such terms as "gang" and "known to be a member" were unacceptably vague. The Court responded in part by noting that, "No man may be required at peril of life, liberty or property to speculate as to the meaning of penal statutes."

Suffice it to say that the void for vagueness doctrine cannot be interpreted quite so simply. To begin with, Hall et al. (1976: 41) provide sound advice in this regard when they caution students of law that, "One must not ride these terms [vagueness, ambiguity, and overbreadth] too hard when reading the [relevant] cases and should remember that most legal terms, unlike those of the physical sciences, are to some extent vague or ambiguous." As a matter of legal theory it is routine to refer to "ordinary citizens," "men of common intelligence," and so on. One is often left with the impression that any literate person should be able to obtain a copy of any criminal code and then, through the exercise of nothing beyond normal diligence, fully appreciate the nature of any conduct that is required or prohibited. In fact, unfortunately, no impression could be further removed from reality. Skilled criminal lawyers routinely differ with one another in their interpretations of legal requirements and prohibitions. The rest of us are doomed almost as soon as we open the criminal code of any jurisdiction. However, our confusion and frustration is not sufficient cause for a particular law to be declared invalid for reasons of vagueness.

Secondly, the appearance of vagueness is often insufficient legal evidence of vagueness. A common and routine practice in our courts is, in effect, an effort to sharpen the focus of otherwise vague provisions of law by adding bits and pieces of what is often referred to as *judicial gloss.* To the extent that past judicial interpretations of the meaning of such otherwise objectionable provisions of a law permits a satisfactory clarification, then the statute in question escapes the void for vagueness doctrine. This point is well-illustrated by *Wainwright v. Stone*, 414 U.S. 21 (1973). Stone, who had been convicted under a Florida statute that prohibited the "abominable and detestable crime against nature," urged the Court to overturn his conviction and to hold that this Florida law was excessively vague. The complaint is easily understood. Absent some clearer statutory language—and there was none—who is to say whether a given act is or is not "abominable and detestable" or a "crime against nature"?

The United States Supreme Court rejected this challenge and noted that the Florida Supreme Court historically had construed the arguably vague statutory language to mean acts of oral or anal intercourse. Judicial interpretation, in other words, had transformed an excessively ambiguous statute into what in practice had quite a specific meaning (but for a quite different disposition of an analogous case, see *Gooding v. Wilson*, 405 U.S. 518 [1972]).

Finally, many void for vagueness challenges in recent decades have prevailed not purely because the appellate courts have objected to ambiguity and vagueness but because of the arbitrary or discriminatory manner in which law enforcement officers chose to apply the challenged statutes. Perhaps the leading case that illustrates this dimension of the void for vagueness doctrine is *Papachristou v. City of Jacksonville*, 405 U.S. 156 (1972). Challenged in *Papachristou* was a Jacksonville ordinance that defined as vagrants "Rogues and vagabonds, or dissolute persons who go about begging, common gamblers, persons who use juggling or unlawful games and plays . . . common night walkers . . . wanton and lascivious persons . . . persons wandering or strolling around from place to place without any lawful purpose or object, habitual loafers" and a broad array of others. The facts in *Papachristou* made it quite obvious that Jacksonville police officers had taken advantage of the vague language of the ordinance to apply the law in a racially discriminatory fashion. Although quickly recognizing the unconstitutional vagueness of the Jacksonville ordinance, Justice Douglas, delivering the opinion of the Court, went on to observe that "Another aspect of the ordinance's vagueness appears when we focus, not on the lack of notice given a potential offender, but on the effect of the unfettered discretion it places in the hands of Jacksonville police" and that "Where, as here, there are no standards governing the exercise of the discretion granted under the ordinance, the scheme permits and encourages an arbitrary and discriminatory enforcement of the law." In such cases it seems clear that the Court is not relying upon the void for vagueness doctrine as a means of pushing for better law or even of upholding the notice doctrine. Instead, the doctrine becomes a means of imposing judicial discipline of law enforcement personnel who are believed to have abused the discretionary powers vested in their positions.

The Double Jeopardy Limitation

Most commentators would define double jeopardy as a topic that deserves consideration in discussions of constitutional limits on the application of criminal law (that is, the law of criminal procedure). Although we agree with that categorization, our concern here is with fundamental limitations on how the state can use the body of criminal law that it creates. This focus creates some gray areas. On one end of the continuum one can find purely procedural issues that have to do with the processes by means of which the state goes about applying the provisions of criminal law. What are the limitations we have placed on law enforcement officials and those acting on behalf of law enforcement officials as they seek evidence to support criminal prosecutions? At what points in the criminal justice process does a defendant's right to counsel emerge? Under what circumstances does a defendant have a constitutionally protected right to trial by jury? At the other end of the continuum are "pure" issues of substantive criminal law. What sorts of conduct can the state define as crimes? What are the critical elements in the definition of a crime? Somewhere toward the center of such a continuum are a set of concerns that can be thought of as being relevant to both substantive criminal law and the law of criminal procedure. One such issue has to do with definitions of those who can be the objects of criminal law. Who, given prevailing provisions of law and constitutional interpretations, is eligible to be prosecuted?

There are many categories of persons who, although they may well have intentionally violated the provisions of soundly constructed criminal laws, are ineligible for prosecution. Most if not all jurisdictions forbid the criminal prosecution of at least some categories of juvenile offenders and require instead that they be brought before juvenile courts. A defendant whose mental status is such that he lacks a "sufficient present rational ability to consult with his lawyer with a reasonable degree of rational understanding . . . [or a] rational as well as factual understanding of the proceedings against him" may not be placed on trial for any criminal offense so long as that mental condition persists (*Dusky v. United States*, 362 U.S. 402 [1960]). Several types of alleged offenders are ineligible for prosecution because, whether before or after the time of the alleged offense, they were granted immunity from prosecution (for instance, diplomatic immunity and witness immunity). These topics will be discussed in Chapter 5. The discussion here should be taken as little more than a single illustration of how the scope of criminal law may be limited by virtue of some persons—as opposed to some acts or definitions of acts—being beyond its reach. It appears in this chapter purely because the double jeopardy prohibition is explicitly stated in the Bill of Rights.

Specifically, the basic constitutional prohibition against double jeopardy may be found in the following portion of the Fifth Amendment: "nor shall any person be subject for the same offense to be twice put in jeopardy of life or limb." The fairly obvious rationale for the limitation is to preclude "repeated attempts to convict a person for an alleged offense, thereby subjecting him to embarrassment, expense and ordeal and compelling him to live in a continual state of anxiety and insecurity as well as enhancing the possibility that even though innocent, he may be found guilty" (*Green v. United States,* 355 U.S. 184, 188 [1957]). Substantially the same objective is sought in civil law by the doctrine of *res judicata* (see, for example, Casad, 1976). This civil law doctrine prohibits the relitigation of matters that have been disposed of previously by an appropriate court and, in effect, accomplishes many of the same purposes in the area of private law that the double jeopardy prohibition accomplishes in the criminal law arena.

Taken out of context, it might well appear that the double jeopardy limitation would have given rise to few problems of interpretation or application. Studiously avoid accepting so simple an image of this limitation on the application of criminal law. Even the present members of the United States Supreme Court have noted the ambiguity that runs through its prior efforts to interpret this important constitutional provision. In *United States v. Scott*, 437 U.S. 82 (1978), for instance, Justice Rehnquist observed that prior decisions of the Court could "hardly be characterized as models of consistency and clarity."

Problems of interpretation notwithstanding, it can be said that the double jeopardy limitation is such that a given political sovereign does not have the constitutional right to place the same defendant twice in jeopardy for the same criminal act. Care must be taken, however, to understand what is meant by such critical terms in the previous sentence as "given political sovereign," "jeopardy," and "same criminal act." First, under our system of government we routinely encounter two sovereign political powers: the federal government and the government of the particular state that may claim jurisdiction over an offense. Importantly, subdivisions of a state (for instance, county or city governmental bodies that may have the power to make limited types of laws) are treated as extensions of the state rather than as "separate sovereigns." It is well established that neither the federal government nor the government of a given state may place a defendant in jeopardy more than once for the same offense (for example, *Green, v. United States,* 355 U.S. 184 [1957]; *Benton v. Maryland,* 395 U.S. 784 [1969]). It is also well established that a state may not place a defendant in jeopardy if that defendant already has been placed in jeopardy for what amounts to the same offense by some political subdivision of that state (see, for instance, *Waller v. Florida,* 397 U.S. 387 [1970; *Brown v. Ohio,* 432 U.S. 161 [1977]; and *Harris v. Oklahoma,* 433 U.S. 682 [1977]). However, what if the same criminal offense is said to offend the criminal law of two different sovereign political powers? What if, for instance, an offender standing in Florida fires a rifle shot that kills a victim standing in Georgia? And what if an offender engages in the armed robbery of a bank in California, obviously a criminal offense in that state, when that bank is federally insured, which has the affect of making his or her offense a violation of federal law? Is only one trial permitted?

As a matter of federal constitutional law, the answers to these questions require that we say that the defendants could be prosecuted by, respectively, both Florida and Georgia and by both California and the federal government (see, for instance, *Bartkus v. Illinois,* 359 U.S. 121 [1959]; *Petite v. United States,* 361 U.S. 529 [1960]; *United States v. Wheeler,* 435 U.S. 313 [1978]). However, this conclusion must be followed with two quick qualifications. First, we state our opinion regarding multiple prosecutions by different states with many misgivings and qualifications. Indeed, only recently the United States Supreme Court agreed to review precisely such a situation in the case of *Heath v. Alabama* (Dockett No. 84-5555 and argued before the Court on October 9, 1985). Thus, this difficult problem may be resolved in the relatively immediate future. Second, it should be understood that the federal government will not initiate a prosecution when the defendant already has been prosecuted by one of the states unless the circumstances are quite unusual. Whether by virtue of state statutes or of state constitutional provisions, multiple prosecutions by states of the same defendant for the same offense—especially when an initial prosecution proved to be unsuccessful—are commonly made unlikely or altogether impossible.

Second, those unfamiliar with criminal law and criminal procedure often arrive at incorrect understandings of what is meant by the jeopardy portion of the double jeopardy prohibition. Some think, for example, that a defendant cannot be twice arrested for the same offense. More are of the opinion that a given case cannot be twice presented to a grand jury or that a given defendant cannot be twice charged with the same offense.

None of these understandings is accurate. It is firmly established that jeopardy only attaches when, in instances of jury trials, the jury has been sworn, or, in instances of bench trials, when the first bit of evidence has been heard (for instance, *Serfass v. United States*, 420 U.S. 377 [1975] and *Crist v. Bretz,* 437 U.S. 28 [1978]). When, as in the vast majority of cases, the defendant enters a plea of guilty and there is no trial, jeopardy attaches when the plea of guilty is accepted by the court. Thus, although defendants cannot be subjected to improper harassment or embarrassment by prosecutors who seek to badger them time after time, more than a single arrest, charge, or presentment of a case to a grand jury is not forbidden by the double jeopardy provision. Furthermore, the limitation does not have the effect of preventing a retrial of a defendant whose appeal of his or her initial conviction is successful (*United States v. Ball,* 163 U.S. 622 [1896]) or of the defendant receiving a harsher sentence when such a retrial takes place (for example, *North Carolina v. Pearce,* 395 U.S. 711 [1969]). It should be noted here that the prosecution may not seek a retrial of a defendant in any appeal filed after such a defendant has been found not guilty (for example, *United States v. Wilson,* 420 U.S. 332 [1975]).

Finally, the limitation does not preclude either situations in which the prosecution files an appeal aimed at the sentence imposed upon a defendant who is convicted at trial (for instance, *United States v. DeFrancesco*, 449 U.S. 17 [1980]) or situations involving defendants whose subsequent sentence is harsher than the one imposed initially (see, for example, *North Carolina v. Pearce*, 395 U.S. 711 [1969] and *Blackledge v. Perry*, 417 U.S. 21 [1974]). The only noteworthy limitation on this general rule was announced by the United States Supreme Court in *Bullington v. Missouri*, 451 U.S. 430 (1980). There the Court held that a defendant not sentenced to death in his initial trial could not receive a sentence of death on retrial without such a sentence being inconsistent with the double jeopardy limitation.

Third, much confusion exists over the phrase "same criminal offense." The old and general rule is that two offenses are not different from one another if the factual proof the state must offer for them is the same (for instance, *Morey v. Commonwealth*, 108 Mass. 433 [1871], *Blockburger v. United States*, 284 U.S. 299 [1932], and *Brown v. Ohio*,

432 U.S. 161 [1977]). The rule is commonly referred to as the *same evidence test* and is the primary standard now in use by most jurisdictions.

The same evidence test, however, poses a variety of troublesome problems. Assume, for instance, that a defendant is charged with murder because he was alleged knowingly to have placed an explosive device on a commerical airliner with the effect that 50 persons lost their lives and that the defendant was acquitted at trial for the murder of only one of those persons. Could he be charged with the murder of other passengers? Perhaps it would seem that this would be permitted. Such a charge would require at least one bit of new evidence (that is, the identity of at least one different victim). The United States Supreme Court has tried to come to grips with this thorny problem several times. Rather than adopting the same evidence test, which would have the effect of asking whether a given offense grew out of "a single criminal act, occurrence, episode, or transaction" (Justice Brennan, dissenting opinion in *Ashe v. Swenson*, 397 U.S. 453, 454 [1970]), the Court seems to have adopted what is referred to as the *principle of constitutional collateral estoppel* for criminal cases.

Perhaps stated too simply, collateral estoppel prohibits the relitigation of facts that have previously been fully considered by a competent court. In the example of the bombing of the commercial airliner, for instance, one might apply the collateral estoppel doctrine by contending that any additional prosecutions of the defendant should be prohibited because all relevant disputed facts already have been resolved in favor of the defendant. If he were found not guilty when tried for the death of one passenger, then how could he possibly be guilty of murdering another passenger who died on the same flight because of the same bombing? In light of the holding of the Court in *Ashe v. Swenson*, it is probable that the collateral estoppel doctrine would be applied to these facts and in favor of the defendant. We should note, however, that the outcome would be quite different had the initial trial resulted in a finding of guilt (see, for instance, *Harris v. Washington*, 404 U.S. 55 [1971]).

The Cruel and
Unusual Punishment Clause

The vast majority of the constitutional problems one encounters in the areas of substantive criminal law and criminal procedure stems from various provisions of the First, Fourth, Fifth, Sixth, and Eighth Amendments (and also, of course, the due process and equal protection clause of the Fourteenth Amendment). Few, if any, of those provisions seem so simple but are in fact so complex as the Eighth Amendment's prohibition against the imposition of any cruel or unusual punishment.

The common problem materializes in those criminal laws that seek to preserve the peace, to prevent crime, or to protect the moral standards of the citizenry in a fashion that is arguably too zealous. Examples would surely include efforts to deal with such concerns as vagrancy, prostitution, homosexuality, drug addiction, alcoholism, and many more situations that pose grave problems of definition of the type we considered when dealing with the void for vagueness and overbreadth doctrines. The temptation is often to push these problems aside by seeking to define those who are, for instance, vagrants or drug addicts as persons who are guilty of a criminal offense rather than seeking to convict some defendants on alleged violations of criminal law associated with such acts (for instance, solicitation for the purpose of prostitution, possession of narcotics, and so on).

Consider, for example, the very important case of *Robinson v. California*, 370 U.S. 660 (1962). Robinson had been convicted under the provisions of a California statute that said to "be addicted to the use of narcotics" was a criminal offense. Robinson was not convicted on charges involving efforts to procure narcotics, unlawful possession of narcotics, or any other behavior associated with the use of narcotics. He was instead convicted because sufficient evidence was introduced to show that he was a person addicted to narcotics (in other words, the status of being a narcotic addict). In this landmark case the Court held that Robinson's punishment was a cruel and unusual sentence of the type prohibited by the Eighth Amendment.

Unfortunately, interpreting *Robinson* and subsequent cases is not a simple matter. If there is a simple interpretation, then it is this: As a fundamental requirement of substantive criminal law, all criminal statutes must contain an *actus reus* element in their definitions. In other words, criminal law must clearly establish the specific nature of the conduct that is either required or prohibited. If, as in *Robinson*, one encounters a law that focuses exclusively on what a person is and not at all on what that person has done or neglected to do, then that criminal law cannot be permitted to stand. Subsequent to *Robinson*, for example, this principle was restated in *Powell v. Texas*, 392 U.S. 514 (1968). Powell had been convicted of public drunkenness. On appeal to the United States Supreme Court, Powell contended that his sentence was a cruel and unusual punishment of the type prohibited by *Robinson*. His public drunkenness, like Robinson's addiction to narcotics, was, he claimed, the direct product of a disease (his alcoholism and Robinson's compulsion to use narcotics). The Court, however, quickly distinguished the two cases by noting that Robinson had been convicted in the absence of any conduct (that is, for the status of being a narcotic addict) whereas Powell's conviction had been premised in part on his unlawful behavior (in other words, appearing in public while intoxicated). Powell's conviction was then affirmed.

So much for the relatively easy issues presented by *Robinson* and *Powell.* The more difficult issues, some of which will draw our attention in chapter 6, concern the voluntariness of Robinson's addiction and Powell's public drunkenness. Albeit with a host of exceptions, the general principle one finds in substantive criminal law is that to be criminal conduct must be voluntary. If otherwise criminal conduct, for instance, is shown to be entirely involuntary in some ordinary use of that term (you slip on an icy sidewalk and in so doing inadvertently strike and cause harm to another) or involuntary in some more limited definitional sense (you take the life of another as a direct consequence of a mental disease or disorder that fully but incorrectly convinces you that the other person is trying to take your life), then it is generally believed that you should not be held criminally liable.

Thought of in this fashion, reconsider *Powell.* If it were shown to be true that he was an alcoholic and that this condition deprived him of the ability to choose between drinking or abstaining from drinking, then should he be held criminally liable for an episode of public drunkenness? Was he morally blameworthy? Should criminal penalties be reserved exclusively for those who can be shown to be morally blameworthy?

There are no easy answers to these questions. Some, however, would adopt the position taken by Justice Fortas who, dissenting in *Powell,* suggested that, "*Robinson* stands upon a principle which, despite its subtlety, must be simply stated and respectfully applied because it is the foundation of individual liberty and the cornerstone of the relations between a civilized state and its citizens: Criminal penalties may not be inflicted upon a person for being in a condition he is powerless to change" (*Powell v. Texas,* 392 U.S. 567 [1968]).

Powerful and persuasive language, but also consider the other side of this very difficult constitutional fence. It is pushed into fairly sharp relief by *United States v. Moore,* 486 F.2d 1139 (D.C. Circuit, 1973), *cert. denied,* 414 U.S. 980 (1974). Moore was convicted on charges involving his unlawful possession of heroin and on appeal contended that his conduct was the involuntary product of his "overpowering need" for heroin. Judge Wilkey, writing for the majority of the court who found Moore's claims unconvincing, wonders aloud regarding where the line would be drawn were Moore's claims to be accepted. Would addicts but not recreational users of drugs be beyond the reach of criminal law because the former were said to be unable to control their conduct? Would such a limitation on criminal law go only to relatively minor offenses like those associated with efforts to purchase and to then possess drugs? If so, then how would one handle the addict who engaged in prostitution, burglary, armed robbery, of a host of larceny offenses purely because the compelling need for drugs drove them to such means of obtaining the necessary funds?

In short, it may be true that cases of the type illustrated here by *Robinson* and *Powell* point to the placement of a constitutional limitation on the reach of criminal law by imposing an *actus reus* as a minimum requirement for statutory constructions. Considered in the broader context of the meaning of the cruel and unusual punishment clause of the Eighth Amendment, however, such cases present us with complex problems of both law and morality while providing few if any acceptable solutions to the many issues neither we nor the courts have yet resolved.

SUMMARY

The central purpose of this chapter has been to show that there are a variety of constitutionally-based limitations that place constraints on the state when it seeks to define actions (or inactions) as crimes and when it seeks to prosecute persons for violations of its criminal law. For instance, the state may not prosecute a defendant for some action or inaction that was not defined as an offense at the time of the act or failure to act. Determinations of who is or is not an offender must be made by the judicial branch of government—and never by the legislative branch. At least in theory, the law must be drafted in such a way as effectively to place all citizens on notice regarding the specific nature of the conduct that is being required or prohibited. No law may limit the free exercise of constitutionally protected behavior (for example, freedom of speech, religion, and so on), and there is a heavy burden of proof on the state if and when it seeks to subject only some segments of the citizenry to the provisions of a given criminal law. Furthermore, the state does not enjoy the power to prosecute any citizen repeatedly or to prosecute even a single time those who have engaged in no prohibited behavior (though it should be recalled that either physical or verbal behavior can stand as the *actus reus* element of a criminal offense).

To be sure, too much can be and sometimes is made of these and other limitations on the power of the State. Constitutional language and interpretations of it often suggest in misleadingly glowing language that ours is a system of law rather than of men and that it is firmly committed to protecting the rights of all citizens to due process and equal protection of law. Too often such language proves to be little more than pleasing but impotent rhetoric. It can make us feel very comfortable without demanding that we do much of anything. Often it provides a semantic shield that masks raw abuses of governmental power, abuses of prosecutorial and judicial discretion, and the perpetuation of a system of social control that preserves the advantages of some at the expense of many.

On the other hand, the alternative of having no lofty principles to which we attribute great ethical, moral, and legal significance is singularly unattractive. The "war against crime" is in many ways akin to a game—a game that is often played with great seriousness and grave consequences. Many of the rules of that game are either stated in or derived from the language of the Constitution. As in all games, violations of rules are to be found, and they often result in no successful claim of the rules having been violated. Yet rules still stand as a benchmark against which we can compare what is with what should be, and rules are adhered to far more often than they are violated. Consequently, the constitutional standards we have reviewed ought not be dismissed as trivial.

DISCUSSION QUESTIONS

1. Our legal system attributes much significance to the idea that law should be stated in language that adequately and effectively places all citizens on notice regarding the nature of the conduct required or prohibited by criminal law. In fact, however, our criminal codes contain vast numbers of complex provisions that even the best-qualified attorneys sometimes find impossible to comprehend. What could or should be done about this problem? How can we, on the one hand, claim that ignorance of the requirements of law is almost never a sound legal defense whereas, on the other hand, we know that no more than a tiny fraction of citizens really appreciate what the law requires or prohibits?

2. Why should the state be prohibited from prosecuting a person who has been found not guilty of a criminal offense if new evidence regarding that offense only comes to light after the initial and unsuccessful prosecution?

5

ESTABLISHING JURISDICTION OVER
OFFENSES AND OFFENDERS

It is firmly established that ours is an accusitorial system of criminal justice. Contending that it has been offended by unlawful conduct or failure to engage in required conduct, the state accuses a defendant of some violation of criminal law. The state—and never the accused defendant—then must bear the full burden of proving beyond a reasonable doubt that its accusation is valid. In no other context do we find any higher standard of proof being applied. Consider, for example, the instructions used in Florida in all criminal cases in an effort to educate members of trial juries regarding the meaning of the "beyond reasonable doubt" language (Florida Standard Jury Instructions in Criminal Cases, Section 2.03):

> A reasonable doubt is not a possible doubt, a speculation, imaginary or forced doubt. Such a doubt must not influence you to return a verdict of not guilty if you have an abiding conviction of guilt. On the other hand, if, after carefully considering, comparing and weighing all the evidence, there is not an abiding conviction of guilt, or, if, having a conviction, it is one which is not stable but one which wavers and vacillates, then the charge is not proved beyond every reasonable doubt and you must find the defendant not guilty because the doubt is reasonable... A reasonable doubt as to the guilt of the defendant may arise from the evidence, conflict in the evidence or lack of evidence.

Furthermore, the state is not permitted to make any effort to shift any portion of its burden of proof to the defendant by, for instance, imposing some requirement that he or she appear as a witness in any criminal court (*Malloy v. Hogan*, 378 U.S. 1 [1964]) or by encouraging the trial judge or jury to draw any inference of guilt from the defendant's refusal to testify (*Griffin v. California*, 380 U.S. 609 [1965], but interested readers should compare *Griffin* with *Donnelly v. DeChristoforo*,

416 U.S. 637 [1974]). This limitation, which is derived from the Fifth Amendment of the Constitution (*Benton v. Maryland*, 395 U.S. 784 [1969]), is emphasized in criminal prosecutions. Again referring to provisions of Florida law, for example, one of two alternative jury instructions is given routinely. In the event that the defendant elects to testify in his or her own behalf, then the members of the jury are told that they "should apply the same rules to consideration of his testimony that you apply to the testimony of other witnesses" (Florida Standard Jury Instructions in Criminal Cases, Section 2.04[c]). When the defendant rejects the opportunity to testify, then care is employed by the trial court judge to avoid members of the jury drawing improper inferences from that decision (Florida Standard Jury Instructions in Criminal Cases, Section 2.04[d]):

> The constitution requires the State to prove its accusations against the defendant. It is not necessary for the defendant to disprove anything. Nor is the defendant required to prove his innocence. . . . The defendant exercised a fundamental right by choosing not to be a witness in this case. You must not view this as an admission of guilt or be influenced in any way by his decision. No juror should ever be concerned that the defendant did or did not take the witness stand to give testimony in the case.

Often, in short, a sound strategy for those accused of criminal acts is to enter a plea of not guilty and to then sit by quite passively. This strategy, however, is but one of a very large number of options that is available. They can and quite commonly do join the battle by asserting one or more justifications, defenses, and excuses. Indeed, a major objective of criminal defense attorneys is to identify the defenses that best fit their clients' cases and to thereby elevate significantly the burden that must be shouldered by the state. Identifying such defenses and reaching some understanding of how they are evaluated when they are raised is at once to enter one of the most intriguing and most complex areas of criminal law.

As we selectively approach this area of law in the balance of this chapter and in chapter 6, it is absolutely essential that the reader keep some of the limitations of our discussion in mind at all times. First, of course, the sheer brevity of the discussion is such that we will be painting with an awfully broad brush. Many matters that would be of great significance to a trial attorney will necessarily escape attention altogether.

Second, subtle as well as major differences in the availability of many defenses and also of how those defenses are to be evaluated exist when the standards of one jurisdiction are compared with those of other jurisdictions. It is imperative that you seek out the particular provisions of law that are applicable to any jurisdiction(s) regarding which you may have some special academic or personal interest.

Finally, various forms of the word "arguable" provide a common denominator for much legal reasoning in this and a host of other areas. This or that defense may arguably be the best defense available to a given defendant in a given criminal case, but being arguably sound is not be to equated with being successful. All defenses are at their core theories regarding why a specific defendant should not be prosecuted or, if prosecuted, not be found guilty of a specific act or combination of acts. Some theories are better than others. Their quality, however, is ultimately to be assessed by the combat that takes place in our trial and our appellate courts.

Though this reality is perhaps unfortunate from the vantage point of those who adhere to abstract principles of justice, a "good defense theory" is seldom to be evaluated in terms of its conceptual or logical elegance. It is instead the theory that prevails on one day in one courtroom and for one defendant. True, it is often said that ours is a legal system within which great reverence is attributed to the principle of *stare decisis*. However, when one steps from the elegant and sometimes esoteric world of legal theory to the practical world of the courtrooms within which theory is translated into practice, one often finds that *stare decisis* is a castle built upon little more than the sands of judicial preference. Thus, any who seek to generalize from one tangible outcome to what is likely to be the outcome in substantially similar future cases must do so at their own risk or that of their clients. Such is the inherent nature of our "trial by combat" system of criminal justice. The objectively stronger party to the combat will usually—but not invariably—be the winner. Stated only somewhat differently, defendants in criminal cases have a constitutionally protected right to a fair and impartial trial, but no right, if some "essential definition" of the term is relied upon, to a flawlessly correct outcome has ever been asserted.

Perhaps we can best begin by observing that there are acts (and also actors) that are in some arguable fashion simply beyond the reach of law or that are at least beyond the reach of the application of law being attempted with regard to a specific act (or actor). Some roughly analogous situations were discussed in adequate detail in Chapter 4. There we saw that a provision of criminal law may run afoul of the void for vagueness doctrine, be overbroad in its construction, violate the constitutional prohibition against *ex post facto* laws, and so on. Similarly, it may be argued that the state, having once unsuccessfully placed a defendant in jeopardy, cannot seek an opportunity for a second prosecution. In these and related settings it is fair to say that defendants are beyond the reach of the law in the sense that efforts at prosecution initiated by the state are in violation of fundamental constitutional principles. There are a variety of other circumstances, however, that may place defendants in substantially the same position.

Some of the more salient of these circumstances deserve discussion here. One obvious illustration of how one might be "beyond the reach of law" involves various contentions that a given court lacks jurisdiction over *either* a particular offense *or* a particular defendant. Such contentions can and often do present us with exceedingly difficult and sometimes very ambiguous problems of law (e.g., Gardner and Manian, 1980: 175-208; Perkins and Boyce, 1982: 38-45). Here, however, we will limit our attention to two general questions. First, when can a given jurisdiction claim successfully that its courts have the right to consider an alleged violation of law? Second, if it can be established that a jurisdiction does have the legal power to consider evidence of relevance to an alleged offense, then does that "jurisdictional reach" attach itself to all persons who might be said to be defendants? Our inquiry will extend beyond these two issues when we reach chapter 6. There we will address only one quite general question: Are there some persons who arguably have engaged in unlawful conduct of a type that properly falls within the jurisdiction of a given court and who enjoy no special immunity from criminal prosecution who are nonetheless not criminally liable for their acts? Although our answers to these questions will be incomplete, they will at least illustrate several basic points that need to be made.

THE PROBLEM OF JURISDICTION
OVER ALLEGED CRIMINAL ACTS

Theories of Jurisdiction

Ours is a system of criminal law that must somehow contend with the problems posed by our having created many different bodies of criminal law. Each state has the power to enact its own body of criminal law. The federal government enjoys a similar power. Under many circumstances members of the military fall within the reach of the Uniform Code of Military Justice (e.g., *O'Callahan v. Parker*, 395 U.S. 258 [1969]). Federal legislation accords a limited degree of independence to Indian tribal courts (e.g., *United States v. Wheeler*, 435 U.S. 313 [1978]). As we saw when we reviewed the constitutional prohibition against double jeopardy and the so-called "separate sovereign rule," these multiple bodies of criminal law can and do present some real problems in the criminal law arena. Here, however, the narrow concern will be with establishing when an offense falls within the jurisdictional reach of a given body of criminal law.

The "pure case," of course, would be exemplified by a person living within a particular jurisdiction who violated a criminal law of that and of no other jurisdiction. For example, Joe, a 25-year old Texan, enters a bar in Dallas and stabs his wife's male escort with a knife. He subsequently confronts a prosecution for aggravated battery in a Texas criminal court. No obvious jurisdictional problems are presented by such cases. The defendant is a citizen of Texas. He is an adult. Each element of his offense materialized within the state of Texas. The offense in question is not violative of the criminal law established by the federal government (at least not given the facts we have described).

But what if our friend Joe had pursued his plan to do harm to his wife's friend in any of several rather different ways? What if, for example, Joe had waited until the friend returned to his home in Oklahoma and then mailed some potentially lethal device—perhaps a "letter bomb"—to him? Apart from any federal prosecution stemming from such an unlawful use of the mail system, is Joe to be prosecuted in Texas? In Oklahoma? In Texas and Oklahoma? And what if Joe had forced his wife's friend into a car that Joe then drove from Texas to Oklahoma and had stabbed him at some unknown point along the way? Obvious additional problems like kidnapping aside, if it could not be established that the stabbing took place in either Texas or Oklahoma, would this mean that Joe's act of aggravated battery would be beyond the jurisdictional reach of both Texas and Oklahoma?

The general problems raised by the above illustrations have to do with the such legal concepts as *situs* (i.e., the location where a criminal act took place), *venue* (i.e., the particular locality within which a prosecution should be initiated), and *jurisdiction* (i.e., as used here, the identification of the specific body of criminal law whose provisions are said to have been violated). There are several jurisdictional theories that have been advanced (e.g., Perkins and Boyce, 1982: 38-45). By and large, however, American courts have relied upon a *territorial theory* that is commonly augmented by an *in whole or in part* extension.

The effect of a "pure" and an "augmented" territorial theory may be summarized fairly simply. If a criminal act is completed—though not necessarily initiated—within the territorial limits of a jurisdiction, then the courts established by that jurisdiction may consider evidence regarding the criminal act in question under a "pure" territorial theory. This, with some exceptions, was the position advanced under common law. When the territorial theory has been extended by the "in whole or in part" addition via appropriate legislative action, then if any "essential element" of a crime (see Chapter 2) takes place within the territorial limits of the jurisdiction, then those same courts may consider evidence even though the "ultimate harm" materialized in some other jurisdiction. Usually the "essential element" language may be interpreted to mean that evidence sufficient to establish a criminal attempt (e.g., attempted aggravated battery) is available.

Thus, a person who intentionally fired a weapon while standing near the border of one state with the intention of murdering a person standing in an adjacent state with the effect that the object of the shooting was unlawfully killed might only be prosecuted for murder in the state where the victim was struck (an unmodified territorial theory) or in either of the two states (if both had by statute created an "in whole or in part" expansion of their jurisdictional reach). (See Chapter 4 for a discussion of how facts such as these might give rise to multiple prosecutions for the same offense.) Sometimes even broader statutory language is relied upon. In Florida, for example, a defendant may be prosecuted in its criminal courts if the alleged offense "is committed wholly or partly within the state," but Florida also claims the right to prosecute those whose "conduct outside the state constitutes an attempt to commit an offense within the state" (Florida Statutes Annotated, Section 910.005[a] and 910.005[b]).

Such broad jurisdictional claims can give rise to major problems. What would be likely to happen, for instance, were Mike, a resident of Atlanta, Georgia to decide that he was going to murder Linda, his ex-wife and a resident of Miami, Florida, and the following events materialized? Mike goes to an Atlanta bar, announces his plan to murder Linda to two of his friends and indicates that he plans to accomplish his goal by placing a bomb in her automobile. He then procures an appropriate explosive device from an illicit vendor in Atlanta and begins driving toward Miami. His friends, however, inform the authorities in Georgia of Mike's plot to kill Linda. Georgia law enforcement officers arrest Mike before he leaves Georgia and charge him with the unlawful possession of an explosive device. Florida, however, contends that Mike should be prosecuted in Florida for the felony offense of attempted murder. Should Georgia officials agree to extradite Mike so that he can be prosecuted in Florida even though no offense of any kind took place within the sovereign geographical boundaries of Florida? Such an extradition and prosecution would appear to be entirely consistent with present provisions of Florida law, but it would surely illustrate how jurisdictional theories can reach well beyond both a pure and an augmented territorial theory of jurisdiction.

The Role Played by
Statutes of Limitation

There is a good deal more to assertions of jurisdiction over offenses than can be derived from assessments of geographical limitations. Time as well as space are of significance. Although reasonable commentators might well differ over how they would categorize the time dimension, here we will identify one aspect that is of relevance to procedural law and one that is of relevance to substantive criminal law. The former issue is beyond the scope of this monograph. We will simply note that a portion of the Sixth Amendment to the Constitution provides that "in all criminal prosecutions, the accused shall enjoy the right to a speedy and public trial." This procedural protection dates back to substantially similar language in the Magna Carta, and it may be found in relevant provisions of law in all American jurisdictions (*Klopfer v. North Carolina*, 386 U.S. 213 [1967]; *United States v. Marion*, 404 U.S. 307 [1971]; *Barker v. Wingo*, 407 U.S. 514 [1972]; and *Dillingham v. United States*, 423 U.S. 64 [1975]). The latter topic, however, deserves a bit more attention.

Limitations on the jurisdictional rearch of criminal law that flow from *statutes of limitations* are only indirectly associated with the various kinds of speedy trial provisions one finds in procedural law. One major difference between the two is that defendants have a constitutionally protected right to be brought to trial fairly promptly. Any protections afforded by statutes of limitations come not by way of constitutional guarantees but from an "act of grace" by the state. In other words, the state confronts no obligation whatsoever to impose some time limit beyond which it loses the ability to "bring a defendant to justice." Indeed, statutes of limitation quite routinely permit prosecutions for especially serious crimes to be initiated at any point in time. From time to time, for example, evidence of a murder only comes to light many years after the offense was committed. Ordinarily, however, this will in no way weaken the ability of the state to claim that it has the right to initiate a prosecution.

Our general purposes here will be served adequately enough by again relying on the Florida Criminal Code for an illustration. The relevant information is contained in Chapter 775.15. There we find that a prosecution for any offense punishable by death or life imprisonment may begin at any time (i.e., such offenses have no statutes of limitations), that prosecutions for other especially serious felony offenses must be initiated within four years after the offense was committed, that prosecutions for less serious felony offenses must take place within three years of the offense, that prosecutions for serious misdemeanors must commence within two years, and that prosecutions for both less serious misdemeanors and infractions must take place within one year of the offense date.

Although each jurisdiction has the opportunity to define the provisions of any statute of limitations in essentially any fashion that it deems to be appropriate, the Florida scheme is fairly typical. Generally speaking, the more serious the nature of the criminal offense being considered, the longer will be the period of time during which prosecutions may lawfully be commenced. Further, provisions are usually made to extend the time period set forth in statutes of limitation if various "special circumstances" exist. In Florida, for instance, the statute of limitations may be extended for as much as three years if a defendant has been "continuously absent from the state or has no reasonably ascertainable place of abode within the state" (Florida Criminal Code, 775.15[6]).

Before we move on to other concerns, we should inject two important points. First, limitations on the jurisdictional reach of criminal law imposed by statutes of limitations are aimed at controlling the time that elapses between the commission of an offense and the initiation of a prosecution. In the event that evidence regarding a criminal act results in the initiation of a prosecution (i.e., the returning of a grand jury indictment or the filing of a bill of information) within an appropriate time span, then the ability of a defendant to "hide out" for some number of years is largely irrelevant. If the reasonable efforts of the state to continue with the prosecution are inhibited by its inability to apprehend the defendant, the state will not lose its "day in court."

Second, there is at least one procedural issue here that cannot be ignored despite the nonprocedural thrust of our discussion. The issue has to do with drawing a distinction between the Sixth Amendment's guarantee to a speedy trial and the due process guarantees one finds in both the Fifth and Fourteenth Amendments. The United States Supreme Court has described the relevant provisions of the Sixth Amendment as providing "an important safeguard to prevent undue and oppressive incarceration prior to trial, to minimize anxiety and concern accompanying public accusation and to limit the possibility that long delay will impair the ability of an accused to defend himself" (*United States v. Ewell*, 383 U.S. 116, 120 [1966]). However, the Court also has noted that Sixth Amendment rights "would seem to afford no protection to those not yet accused, nor would they seem to require the Government to discover, investigate, and accuse any person within any particular period of time" (*United States v. Marion*, 404 U.S. 307, 313 [1971]).

The apparent inapplicability of Sixth Amendment protections regarding the time that elapses between a criminal act and the initiation of a prosecution, however, does not mean that the state can do whatever it pleases. To begin with, consider the following summary of the objectives of statutes of limitations as they were described in *Toussie v. United States* (397 U.S. 112, 114-115 [1970]).

> The purpose of a statute of limitations is to limit exposure to criminal prosecution to a certain fixed period of time following the occurrence of those acts the legislature has decided to punish by criminal sanctions. Such a limitation is designed to protect individuals from having to defend themselves against charges when the basic facts may have become obscured by the passage of time and to minimize the danger of official punishment because of acts in the far-distant past. Such a time limit may also have the salutary effect of encouraging law enforcement officials promptly to investigate suspected criminal activity.

Because of the obvious significance of these goals, it has been established that "the Due Process Clause of the Fifth Amendment would require dismissal of [indictments] if it were shown at trial that the preindictment delay . . . caused substantial prejudice to . . . rights to a fair trial and that the delay was an intentional device to gain tactical advantage over the accused" (*United States v. Marion*, 404 U.S. 307, 324 [1971]).

In summary, then, the state, whether bound or not bound by statutes of limitations, does not have the option of "sitting on evidence" for as long as it pleases purely because doing so would not trigger the Sixth Amendment rights of a potential defendant. Selecting such an inappropriate strategy can be so offensive to that person's right to due process of law that the state can lose jurisdiction over any offense that person may actually have committed.

THE PROBLEM OF JURISDICTION OVER ALLEGED OFFENDERS

It should now be obvious that being able to establish probable cause that a criminal offense has been committed and that a particular person or persons committed that offense is a necessary but not a sufficient condition to go forward with a prosecution. In other words, although no prosecution is possible unless these two conditions have been satisfied, their having been satisfied is no guarantee that a prosecution will be either possible or successful. Among other things, one must be able to identify that sovereign political entity (that is, the jurisdiction) that properly can claim that it has the power to initiate a prosecution. But the burden we place on the state does not stop with resolving problems associated with jurisdiction over a particular offense. It also must show that it has jurisdiction over the alleged offender(s). Here we will illustrate this burden with reference to three types of defendants: (1) those who are juveniles, (2) those who enjoy some type of diplomatic immunity, (3) those who have been granted legislative immunity, and (4) those who have been granted witness immunity.

The Defense of Infancy or Immaturity

With regard to juveniles, the reader must understand that we have created a most unusual division between our juvenile and our criminal justice systems over the past century and a half (e.g., Krisberg and Austin, 1978; Feld, 1981, 1983; Wadlington et al., 1983; and Thomas and Bilchik, 1985). Contemporary developments in juvenile law are having the practical and legal effect of diminishing the distinctions between juvenile and criminal law in many important as well as highly controversial ways. However, the vast majority of juveniles who are charged with unlawful acts either are not or cannot be prosecuted in any criminal court.

This practice has its roots in two rather separate theories of jurisdiction. One of these reaches far back into our English common law heritage. At common law persons below the age of seven were presumed to lack the capacity to form the intent to commit a criminal act and therefore were entirely immune from prosecution. Persons between the ages of seven and fourteen were "rebuttably presumed" to lack any criminal capacity. In other words, in cases involving these young defendants, the prosecution could introduce evidence aimed at demonstrating that the presumption of incapacity did not apply and, consequently, that the prosecution should be permitted. Persons who were fourteen or older at the time of any alleged offenses were defined as being adults for prosecutorial purposes.

These common law provisions gave rise to the so-called *defense of infancy* or *defense of immaturity*. The defense, of course, can be thought of as an effort to contend that the *mens rea* element one finds in the definitions of most crimes could not be proven by the state. In many ways, however, these common law principles may be equally accurately thought of as limiting the ability of a criminal court to assert a right to prosecute a large category of persons even when there was probable cause to believe that they had engaged in unlawful conduct.

The other theory of jurisdiction regarding juveniles is even more matter-of-fact. During the early decades of this century the push for an entirely separate system of juvenile justice, a movement that began with creation of the House of Refuge in New York City in 1825, gained much momentum. The initial legislation was enacted in Illinois in 1899. By 1945 every jurisdiction in the United States had created some type of separate juvenile court system. Whether by routine practice or by formal provisions of statutory law, these newly established juvenile courts successfully claimed jurisdiction over virtually all cases involving those defined as children. Such defendants, typically any persons below the age of 18, confront petitions alleging that they have engaged in acts of juvenile delinquency and not charges that they have engaged in criminal conduct.

This distinction may seem to be subtle, but it is not. For example, assume that a 13-year old boy is arrested for having stolen a car. Virtually without exception, the boy could not be charged with grand theft auto (in other words, a felony). Instead, a petition would be filed alleging that he was a delinquent child with the evidence of the auto theft being used to prove his delinquency. A significant part of the reason why this would be done has to do with the jurisdictional powers accorded juvenile courts in the United States. Although we are seeing numerous legal devices developing today that undermine the traditional powers granted to juvenile courts, they continue to be granted either *exclusive jurisdiction* over all cases involving juveniles (i.e., they are the only court before whom a juvenile may be brought) or *concurrent jurisdiction* over such cases (i.e., they share jurisdictional powers with the criminal court but do so in such a way that the distinction between exclusive and concurrent jurisdictional powers is largely academic). More importantly for our purposes here, the case of the 13-year old boy would provide a clear illustration of an *offense* that would usually fall within the jurisdiction of a criminal court but an *offender* who is beyond the court's jurisdictional reach.

Diplomatic Immunity as A Defense

Age is not the only variable that can put defendants beyond the jurisdiction of our criminal courts even though those courts normally would assert jurisdiction over the conduct in which they have engaged.

An additional limitation on jurisdiction that recently has attracted a good deal of commentary in the media is that created by *diplomatic immunity*. At least in principle, however, this limitation may be summarized concisely.

As a long-standing provision of international law, foreign diplomats (and also members of their families and many of their employees) are accorded full immunity from criminal prosecution while they are working in the United States (for instance, 22 U.S.C. Section 252). More limited immunity is accorded lower-ranking consular officials. Those persons who enjoy full diplomatic immunity are beyond the jurisdictional reach of either state or federal criminal courts regardless of the nature of their conduct. Those persons granted limited diplomatic immunity are only within the jurisdictional reach of those courts if they have engaged in especially serious offenses. Generally speaking, therefore, the belief that such persons have violated the provisions of state or federal criminal law results only in their forced expulsion from the United States.

The award of diplomatic immunity creates relatively infrequent problems in the area of criminal law. By and large, foreign diplomats are responsible, law-abiding persons who take their duties as governmental representatives quite seriously. Consequently, although they may habitually take advantage of their special status by, for instance, ignoring local traffic and parking laws, their involvement in more significant offenses is minimal. On the other hand, it also is true that situations involving harmful criminal conduct attract much public attention and condemnation. Why, some people often complain, should "these foreigners" enjoy more privileges than do our own citizens?

The only basic response to such complaints is (1) that equal privileges are accorded our own diplomats when they are working in other nations, (2) that awards of diplomatic immunity are an important tool by means of which significant national interests are protected, (3) that foreign governments are unlikely to react in a warm and kindly fashion to any of their representatives who violate our laws, and (4) that the net benefits of diplomatic immunity provisions are far greater than is the harm done by offenders who are beyond the reach of our legal system. However, such responses tend to obscure two important points. First, it ignores how diplomatic immunity removes any and all effective remedies from those who may have been harmed by persons who are immune from prosecution in our courts. Second, it trivializes the fairly obvious fact that some modern nations are hardly definable as "good international citizens." You may recall the fairly recent situation involving a person or persons in a Libyan embassy in England who shot and killed a police officer. One can and perhaps should ask pointed questions regarding whether such offenders, especially when they are representatives of a nation that systematically has shown so little regard for principles of either national or international law, deserve any special protection. (On the other hand, of course, were one to begin to deny such protection, then how would one go about the business of ignoring immunity after it had been granted? Not unlike a variety of freedom of speech and other First Amendment issues, it may be true that diplomatic immunity must either be preserved much as it is today or be abolished altogether.)

Legislative Immunity as a Defense

Awards of *legislative immunity*, although a good deal more limited both in scope and the time span they cover than is the case with full diplomatic immunity, may be thought of as a means by which some persons move beyond the jurisdictional reach of law. Another fundamental distinction between diplomatic and legislative immunity, however, is that the latter is provided for in the body of the federal Constitution and in the constitutional documents of most if not all of the individual states. Regarding the legislative immunity accorded members of the Congress of the United States, for example, Article I, Section 6 of the Constitution makes it clear that those persons "shall in all cases except treason, felony, and breach of the peace, be privileged from arrest during their attendance at the sessions of their respective houses, and in going to and returning from the same . . . "

The purpose of legislative immunity awards, of course, is quite similar to that associated with diplomatic immunity. Those in the executive branch, which includes such law enforcement representatives as police and prosecutors, are prohibited from inappropriately interfering with representatives of the legislative branch as the latter go about the business of discharging their constitutional obligations. One hardly needs to be a historian to identify episodes in the relatively recent constitutional history of the United States that presented a clear and present threat of such interference. Thus, although we need not delve into the issue in any detailed fashion here, the significance of what is in effect a check on the power of the executive branch should not be ignored.

Witness Immunity as a Defense

Finally, quite a different sort of immunity is associated with persons called by state or federal prosecutors to testify in criminal cases. Most commonly this limitation on the jurisdiction of our criminal courts stems from the considerable tension that often develops by, on the one hand, a Fifth Amendment prohibition against any person being required to testify against himself or herself and, on the other hand, a proper desire on the part of the state to prosecute offenders. All states in the nation as well as the federal government now have statutes that permit this tension to be resolved by the granting of *witness immunity* (e.g., *Counselman v. Hitchcock*, 142 U.S. 547 [1892]; *Kastigar v. United States*, 406 U.S. 441 [1971]).

The primary purpose served by awards of witness immunity should be quite apparent. All too often prosecutors find themselves in the position of wanting to initiate a prosecution against a person whom they fully believe is guilty of a criminal offense but hesitating to file charges because they know that the supporting evidence is insufficient. Assume, for instance, that the police have found the body of a murder victim in an all-night convenience store, persuasive evidence that John and Mary were in the neighborhood of the store at the approximate time of the crime, and witnesses who are able to testify that John and Mary were in possession of a large amount of money on the day after the murder. The police, in short, have put together a weak case that would in all probability not support a prosecution either for robbery or murder. Diligent investigative efforts yield no evidence. The prosecutor, however, is convinced that Mary was serving as the driver of a "get-away car" and that John committed both the robbery and the homicide.

Should the prosecutor do nothing simply because a sound case cannot be put together? Perhaps. But what is more likely to happen is that John and Mary will be arrested, both will be charged with robbery and murder, and both will perhaps be told that murder committed during the course of a serious offense is punishable by a sentence of death. And then the prosecutor will have a meeting with Mary and her defense attorney. The time to deal will have arrived. An award of witness immunity is likely to be given to Mary such that she cannot be prosecuted for either the robbery or the murder—on the condition, of course, that she agree to testify against John. (In fact, her agreement is a practical rather than a legal matter. Once an award of witness immunity is granted, then the person receiving that grant has no legal right to refuse to answer all questions and to answer them honestly. To refuse to testify would be to be in contempt of court; to testify dishonestly rather than honestly is to invite prosecution for perjury—the one criminal offense for which witness immunity provisions provide no protection whatsoever (e.g., *United States v. Mandujano* 425 U.S. 564 [1974].) Mary, after all, was an eye witness. Mary, we can assure you, is most unlikely to "take her chances" at trial given the awesome consequences of its potential outcome. Mary is quite likely to jump at the opportunity to escape the risk she would otherwise confront. In effect, then, the prosecutor "gives a little to get a little."

Witness immunity statutes, however, must be approached both with care and with an eye to whether they create equal benefits for both the witness who is to provide testimony that would otherwise be impossible to obtain and the prosecutor who is representing the interests of the state. The need for a careful reading of witness immunity provisions of law stems from their falling into either of two quite different categories: *transactional immunity statutes* and *derivative use immunity statutes.*

Under the provisions of a transactional immunity statute there is an absolute bar against any future prosecution of a witness for any offense(s) about which he or she was asked to testify. Thus, for example, the witness would be immune from prosecution even if law enforcement officials subsequently located entirely persuasive evidence regarding the witness's criminality in a way that was entirely independent of any testimony the witness provided about such unlawful conduct. This would not be true, however, under provisions of law that grant derivative use immunity (e.g., *Kastigar v. United States*, 406 U.S. 441 [1972]). If the prosecution can shoulder the burden of proving that evidence being used against a defendant who was previously granted this type of immunity was not in any way derived from the testimony of that witness, then the prior award of immunity will not prohibit the prosecution of the "witness turned defendant."

Apart from problems posed by the "scope" of the immunity that has been granted, there is also something of a fairness issue that should not be ignored. Until fairly recently awards of immunity to potential witnesses were primarily a means by which the prosecution could bolster its position. In other words, immunity was a consequence of an independent determination made by a representative of the executive branch of government (i.e., the prosecutor) rather than, for example, the outcome of a motion made during a trial and ruled upon by a representative of the judicial branch (i.e., the trial court judge). It has not been and is not now a tool that is routinely available to defense attorneys. Although there are some signs today that trial court judges are becoming inclined to extend judicial immunity to defense witnesses under some fairly extreme circumstances, the imbalance of power that has been in evidence for many years is most unlikely to be remedied in the future.

SUMMARY

Our goal in this chapter has been to build upon materials addressed in Chapter 2, which reviewed the essential elements of crimes and established the need for the state to prove each element by a beyond reasonable doubt standard, and Chapter 4, portions of which identified important limitations on the "reach" of criminal law. In particular, we sought to emphasize that having a constitutionally sound criminal law and being able to contend that such a law has been violated by a particular defendant are but two of many dimensions of what is involved in a criminal prosecution.

To begin with, one encounters problems in attempting to claim that a particular jurisdiction has the legal right to initiate a prosecution in reaction to a particular offense. Our illustrations have shown that such problems can stem from *both* the physical location of the offense *and* from the time period that elapses between the offense and the initiation of a prosecution. Other than difficulties that may materialize when a given offense is said to be in violation of provisions of both federal and state criminal law, the physical location of a crime is not a significant issue. However, when an offense begins in one jurisdiction and ends in another jurisdiction—and sometimes when all relevant elements of an offense materialize in one jurisdiction with the objective of completing the offense in another jurisdiction—significant disputes do occur. The general principle one most commonly encounters is provided by what we described as a territorial theory of jurisdiction that has been augmented by an "in whole or in part" standard, but exceptions even to that fairly broad principle were noted.

Secondly, we observed that statutes of limitations can place temporal limits on jurisdiction over criminal offenses. Care, of course, must be taken to distinguish between the role played by statutes of limitations and the rights defendants enjoy because of the speedy trial guarantee set forth in the Sixth Amendment. The individual states may not undermine the right of a defendant to be placed on trial promptly after a prosecution has been initiated, but the states have no constitutional obligation to enact statutes of limitations. On the other hand, we noted that the discretion accorded the states and the federal government with regard to statutes of limitations does not mean that prosecutors can delay filing charges as long as they wish or until they feel that they have gained some tactical advantage over defendants. Intentional delays can be defined as a violation of defendants' rights to due process of law under the terms of the Fifth and the Fourteenth Amendment, and violations of those rights can result in the dismissal of all charges brought by a prosecutor who does not move forward with his or her case in a reasonably diligent fashion.

Finally, we have seen that there is more to jurisdictional problems than variables associated with space and time. One also must carefully consider the possibility that our criminal courts may lack jurisdiction over the person who is believed to have violated some provision of criminal law. Our illustrations showed that jurisdiction may be lost because of the age of the offender (i.e., the defense of infancy or immaturity), the political status of the offender (i.e., diplomatic and legislative immunity), and the ability of the offender to claim that he or she is beyond the reach of the court because of his or her having received an award of judicial or prosecutorial immunity (i.e., witness immunity).

It will soon become apparent that the ability of the state to claim jurisdiction over an offense and an offender is but a preliminary concern. Those charged with criminal offenses in our system of justice have access to a variety of means by which they can contend that what was done ought not be defined as a crime or that what was done ought to be excused. Many of those so-called justifications, defenses, and excuses will draw our attention in the following chapter.

DISCUSSION QUESTIONS

1. Under what specific circumstances should persons escape criminal responsibility for their harmful conduct purely because they have expressed a willingness to provide otherwise unavailable testimony? Is justice really to be defined in terms of who could reach the prosecutor first in an effort to "strike a deal"?

2. Should diplomatic officials be accorded full immunity from criminal prosecution? Why? Why not? If full or partial immunity is to be given to such persons, then who should assume the liability for the harm such persons may have caused others? The government of the United States? The government represented by the diplomat? If it is to be the government being represented, then how could a victim demand that damages due him or her be paid?

3. What justification would you offer for the creation of statutes of limitations? What if any difference should there be between protections provided by statutes of limitations and Sixth Amendment rights to a speedy trial?

6

JUSTIFICATIONS, DEFENSES, AND EXCUSES

Much territory has been touched upon in the previous chapters. We have discussed the historical development of law, how criminal law differs significantly from other bodies of law, problems one encounters in the creation of criminal codes, how the application of criminal law is limited with regard both to when our courts can assert jurisdiction over a particular offense and to when they can claim jurisdiction over a particular offender, and a broad array of other concerns. A critically important as well as intriguing area of substantive criminal law, however, has received no more than passing mention. It is quite a general segment of criminal law that has to do with a diverse set of justifications, defenses, and excuses that defendants in criminal cases can raise in an effort either to shield themselves from conviction (that is, *complete defenses*) or to diminish the seriousness of the offenses for which they are convicted (in other words, *partial* or *incomplete defenses*).

Legal defenses of the types we will soon discuss, of course, are the sorts of things that one encounters quite routinely in media-based fictional or nonfictional accounts of what takes place within our criminal justice system. There is no shortage of well-known illustrations. John Hinkley's shooting of President Reagan was shown time and time again on national television, yet Hinkley escaped being convicted of attempted murder by successfully raising the insanity defense. Virtually everyone in the nation saw videotapes of John DeLorean engaging in what appeared to be a major drug offense and his subsequent contention that the behavior of federal law enforcement officials constituted entrapment. (But you may recall that the defense of entrapment failed to serve the purpose of the so-called Abscam defendants.) And illustrations need not be limited to those involving powerful and influential victims and defendants. Hardly a day passes without a news account of a storekeeper who shot and killed someone who was engaged in an attempted robbery, a homeowner who seriously wounded someone burglarizing his or her home, or a private citizen who "took the law into his own hands" by coming to the aid of someone who was the object of a criminal victimization.

Despite the diverse character of these and many related kinds of situations, they share something of a common denominator. Each involves a person who engaged in some form of conduct that under the vast majority of circumstances would be a clear violation of the provisions of criminal law, but each also involves a real or potential defendant who contended that his or her conduct ought not be defined as criminal. Indeed, in the examples of the storekeeper, the homeowner, and the "good Samaritan," one might well anticipate that they would become the objects of public praise rather than legal condemnation.

Quite a large number of more or less independent justifications, defenses, and excuses are available to defendants who find that their conduct as well as their persons are "within the reach" of criminal law. Those we discuss in the balance of this chapter should be thought of as illustrations and certainly not as an exhaustive list. Additional limitations on what follows—most of which have been noted in earlier chapters—also should be kept in mind very carefully.

First, under many circumstances defendants will avoid confining themselves to only a single defense. Instead, based on their understanding of all relevant facts surrounding the charges that may or have been filed against them, they will "mix and match" as many individual defenses as they can. Thus, you should avoid any temptation to think of particular defenses as ones that necessarily "stand alone."

Second, critically important jurisdictional differences exist regarding the specific defenses that can be asserted and the manner in which available defenses are evaluated. It is imperative that no reader assume that our general discussion can be used as a set of guidelines that describe the legal rights and privileges that exist in any particular jurisdiction.

Finally, as was indicated early in Chapter 5, a defense that prevails in one court for one defendant on one day provides no guarantee whatsoever that the same defense will prevail again even in virtually identical circumstances and in the very same courtroom. As was true in earlier portions of our discussion, we will be talking about legal devices by means of which defendants seek to win the battle in which they find themselves. Despite much effort to establish general rules and guidelines that govern what can or cannot take place on the battlefield of a criminal court, those principles are bent or broken often enough that relying on them to predict trial outcomes is a high risk undertaking that we do not recommend to anyone.

AN OVERVIEW OF COMMON LEGAL DEFENSES

Mistakes of Law and of Fact as Defenses

Consider the following two hypothetical situations.

Susan, while taking an afternoon walk through a state park, comes upon some unusual flowers to which she is very much attracted. She picks several of them to take home to her apartment, but is promptly stopped by a police officer who had been watching her and given a summons requiring her to appear before a municipal court. There was, it turns out, a state law that had been "on the books" for many years that defined as a misdemeanor the very behavior in which Susan had engaged. Susan subsequently appeared in court and testified that she was totally unaware of the applicable city ordinance and only picked the flowers in the public park because she fully believed that doing so was lawful.

John was beginning the fall semester at a large state university and had gone to the campus bookstore to purchase some supplies. Following the policies of the bookstore, he left a red nylon backpack that contained all of his textbooks at the front of the store, purchased the supplies he needed, returned to the front of the store, picked up a red backpack, and walked outside. Less than a block away from the bookstore he was stopped by a campus police officer and a very angry student. The backpack proved to be the property of the angry student and was found to contain both that student's books and a billfold in which there was a significant amount of money. Subsequently charged with the felony offense of grand larceny, John testified at trial that he never intended to steal anything from anyone and had only taken the other student's backpack because he fully believed it to be his own property.

What ought be done with these two cases? Assume that you believe Susan's contention that she is a law-abiding person who only picked the flowers in the park because of her inaccurate belief that such behavior was lawful. Also assume that John really took the valuable property of another student only because he believed that he was taking his own property.

Suffice it to say that these two situations are different from one another because, among other things, Susan raised a *mistake of law* as her defense and John raised *mistake of fact* as his defense. They also are similar in that neither Susan nor John had any real desire or intent to violate any provision of criminal law. Generally speaking, however, Susan really has raised no defense at all. There is a powerful presumption in our system of law that all citizens have full knowledge of the body of criminal law which is in force in their jurisdiction. Only in very exceptional circumstances will true ignorance of law or an honest misunderstanding of law be an effective defense (see, for instance, *Lambert v. California*, 355 U.S. 225 [1957]; *Bouie v. City of Columbia*, 378 U.S. 347 [1964]). True, in everyday life one might reason that Susan's offense was not a real offense because there is no obvious indication of any criminal intent. However, recall the discussion in chapter 2 regarding the *mens rea* element for general intent crimes. Relevant legal theory and practice hold that general intent (as opposed, for example, to specific intent) will be presumed to be a characteristic of the offense purely because of the nature of the conduct.

But John's case differs from Susan's in legally important ways. He did not contend, for instance, that he was ignorant of the fact that larceny was defined as unlawful conduct. Further, his real defense was that he only took what he honestly and reasonably believed to be his own property. Therein lies the legal rationale for excusing John's conduct. Had the facts been what John honestly and reasonably believed them to be, then what he did would not have been unlawful. Naturally, the "honestly and reasonably" phrase is one that requires interpretation given the relevant facts surrounding a given case. For example, John's situation would have been far more difficult had he taken a briefcase rather than a backpack, a green backpack rather than a red backpack, and so on.

In short, whereas mistake of law seldom suffices as a defense in our system of criminal law, mistake of fact has proven to be a good deal more persuasive. Its viability, however, must be evaluated quite carefully and in terms of the elements by means of which a given criminal offense is defined. Consider, for example, the following language from Chapter 794 of the Florida Criminal Code, the section within which several sex offenses are defined:

> When, in this chapter, the criminality of conduct depends upon the victim's being below a certain specified age, ignorance of the age is no defense. *Neither shall misrepresentation of age by such person nor a bona fide belief that such person is over the specified age be a defense* [Emphasis added].

Consequently, an entirely honest and reasonable belief that one's sexual partner was 18 years of age or older would be no defense at all in Florida.

Consent and Condonation as Defenses

Little time need be devoted to the role played—or not played—by *consent* and *condonation* as separate defenses to prosecution beyond the need to distinguish between them. Perhaps the most straightforward distinction is to be found in the fact that always consent exists *prior* to some bit of arguably criminal conduct and condonation develops only *after* such conduct. Consider the following two fact situations.

> After having dated him several times Mary, an adult college student, agrees to have sexual intercourse with George. Later on the very same evening George admits to having a similar relationship with one of Mary's closest friends. Mary, enraged by George's revelation, immediately telephones the police and claims that George raped her. George is promptly arrested and charged with rape.

> Sally, another adult college student, was in her apartment with Lonn, an old friend from her high school days that she had dated fairly frequently. Though Sally verbally and physically resisted Lonn's unwelcome sexual advances, Lonn was ultimately able to force her to have sexual intercourse with him. Sally reported the sexual assault to the police. Lonn returned to Sally's apartment the next morning, apologized profusely for his behavior of the previous evening, and begged her to not testify against him at the trial he feared was certain to take place. Feeling sorry for her old friend despite what he had done to her, Sally finally "gave in" and accepted Lonn's apology.

At least in terms of legal theory, what should happen with regard to George and Lonn? It should be obvious immediately that George should not be prosecuted for the felony offense of rape. The elements of this offense routinely include such terms as the use or threat of force and coercion. The terms do not "fit" George's conduct. Further, of course, there is no indication of any criminal intent on George's part. Although there are limits to the nature of criminal offenses for which the defense of consent is appropriate—it cannot be used, for example, in cases involving criminal homicide—it would be entirely appropriate for George's situation. Mary's consent clearly eliminates the ability of the state to show that the essential elements of the rape offense existed.

Lonn, however, is in a very different situation. He did rely upon physical force; Sally did resist his sexual advances as best she could. Her willingness to forgive him does not give rise to a sound basis for the defense of condonation of the crime by a victim. The general weakness of the defense is well established both as a matter of ancient common law and as a principle of modern law (see, for instance, Perkins and Boyce,

1982: 1088-1092). In principle, then, Lonn committed and should be prosecuted for his rape of Sally. (In fact, of course, were Sally to refuse to cooperate with the prosecution, then there would be little if any probability of Lonn's being put on trial for his criminal act.)

Necessity and Coercion as Defenses

The *defense of necessity* and the *defense of coercion* or *duress* share two important common denominators. First, those advancing them contend that their otherwise criminal conduct should be excused because such conduct was a direct product of forces over which they had no control. Although one does encounter some confusion and inconsistency in some relevant cases, what distinguishes the two defenses is whether such forces are associated with natural events (the defense of necessity) or human acts (the defense of coercion). Second, neither of these defenses will inhibit the prosecution of persons charged with acts of criminal homicide (see, for example, *Regina v. Dudley and Stephens*, 14 Q.B.D. 273 [1884]). (Here we should quickly note that the rationale employed to support either of these defenses might result in a less serious charge or conviction than what would have been encountered otherwise—perhaps voluntary manslaughter rather than first degree murder— and also might be taken into consideration when the time for sentencing arrives.)

In some ways the defense of necessity is the easier of the two to apply in most situations, so we will begin with a brief overview of that defense. As an illustration, consider the following.

> Ron was on a hunting trip in an isolated section of Colorado when he encountered a blizzard. Nearly blinded by the driving snow and fearing that he would soon freeze to death if he failed to find shelter, Ron came across a locked cabin. He broke the lock, entered the cabin, built a fire, and consumed various provisions that had been stored in the cabin while he waited for the storm to abate.

Should Ron be held criminally liable for any of these acts? The answer is that no criminal liability would attach to Ron given the facts as we have described them. Ron was reasonably in fear of physical harm to himself and engaged in only those otherwise criminal acts that were necessary to protect him from the harm he feared. Indeed, it should be noted carefully (1) that the seriousness of the harm from which Ron wished to protect himself was greater than the harm caused by his conduct, (2) that there was a close relationship between the nature of his conduct and the harm he sought to avoid, and (3) that he lacked any meaningful access to lawful means of avoiding harm. The absence of any of these characteristics would erode away the utility of the defense of necessity. A person who becomes thirsty while walking through a residential neighborhood on a sunny afternoon, for example, could hardly use this defense were he or she to break into the house of another and rummage around in search of a cold bottle of beer!

The defense of coercion presents some similar as well as some additional problems. A "pure case" might be described in the following terms.

> Linda was working as a cashier at convenience store when two men approached her. Both were masked and armed with shotguns. One of them demanded that she turn over all of the money in her cash register, and he promised to "blow her away" if she failed to comply with the demand immediately. Fully believing that he would carry through with the promise, Linda did what she was told to do.

Should Linda be held liable for any criminal offense? Of course not. She had no criminal intent; her act was not voluntary. To be sure, criminal liability would certainly attach to Linda were she to simply give a normal customer all of the funds under her control. In this situation, however, she did no more and no less than what she reasonably believed she had to do to protect herself from the immediate risk of death or serious bodily injury. Much like the case of Ron, the immediate harm she sought to avoid was far greater than the offensiveness of what otherwise would have been criminal conduct, what she did was directly related to her reasonable desire to escape harm, and she had no apparent lawful means of avoiding that harm. She clearly acted under extreme duress.

Unfortunately, many who are unfamiliar with the operation of our legal system are inclined to imagine that the defense of coercion has a far broader application than it actually has. Suffice it to say that the defense of coercion is not viable if it is raised by a defendant who (1) has been charged with criminal homicide, (2) was not confronting an immediate risk of death or serious injury, or (3) was responding to a type or degree of coercion that would not intimidate an ordinary citizen. Thus, for example, were someone to mail a letter to you in which he or she threatened to injure you seriously if you did not steal a particular valuable object from your employer and leave the article at a designated place at a designated time, your theft of the article would not be excused by your raising the defense of coercion. The risk of harm would not be immediate. The person applying the coercion would not be confronting you. The opportunity to resolve your fear of harm in various noncriminal ways would certainly exist. In short, you would be in big trouble.

Defense of Self or of Third Persons

The right of private citizens to use lethal or nonlethal force either in defense of themselves or of others is an important although often complex area of criminal law. Our broad overview should therefore be considered with special care and with an appreciation for the fact that we will consider only general principles in this discussion.

The basic standard for evaluating self-defense claims is easily enough summarized. Otherwise blameless persons (and not those who are involved in criminal conduct) generally have the legal right to defend themselves against harm to their persons by relying upon nonlethal force and, if the attack they are confronting carries an immediate threat of serious bodily injury or death, upon lethal force. One may meet force with force, deadly force with deadly force.

In evaluating such claims, the general standards are these: Was the defendant free from fault himself or herself? Was his or her perception of the risk being confronted a reasonable—though not necessarily an accurate—perception under the circumstances that were confronted? Was the type or degree of force upon which he or she relied reasonable in light of the type or degree of force that he or she confronted? Finally, in the many jurisdictions that have adopted a so-called *retreat rule*, was there no safe route of retreat available to the defendant that, had it been pursued, would have precluded his or her need to use the means of self-defense that were in fact relied upon?

If and only if an affirmative answer is possible for each of these questions will the defendant's claim that his or her conduct was justified be accepted (for instance, Hall et al., 1976: 579-605; Fletcher, 1978: 855-875; Inbau et al., 1980: 317-339; and Perkins and Boyce, 1982: 1093-1144). Naturally, the burden on the defendant is increased when his or her conduct moves from the zone of nonlethal to that of lethal force.

The difficulty, of course, comes when judges or juries are called upon to look backward in time, attempt to place themselves in the position of defendants, and then to speculate about what the defendants confronted and whether the defendants' assertions of self-defense are sound defenses. Sometimes the task is handled with relative ease. Witnesses present at the time of relevant events testify that the owner of a store was confronted by an armed assailant, that the assailant fired a shot that wounded the owner, that the owner responded by grabbing a weapon from beside a cash register, and that the assailant was killed by a shot fired by the owner.

All too often, however, the facts introduced are not so crisp and clean. A woman charged with murder contends that she was asleep in her home one evening when she was awakened by a noise in the hallway leading to her bedroom. Claiming that she was horrified by what she believed was an immediate risk either to herself or to her two young children, she grabbed for a large caliber revolver. When the door to her bedroom was pushed open, she fired three shots in rapid succession. The intruder was killed instantly, but was then found to be the woman's husband who had returned from a business trip a day ealier than had been expected. The prosecutor challenges the self-defense claim, which in this illustration is merged with a mistake of fact defense, by introducing evidence that showed that the husband had planned to file for a divorce from his wife and that he had made plans to marry another woman. The prosecutor's theory is that the woman recognized precisely who was in the hallway and simply took advantage of the situation in an effort to thwart her husband's plans as well as to collect a substantial amount of life insurance that would be hers were her defense to be accepted. Whom would you believe were you a member of this hypothetical jury? Why?

The problems become somewhat more complicated as we move from self-defense to *defense of third persons*. Generally speaking, citizens have the right to come to the defense of their fellow citizens and, if they elect to do so, "to meet force with force" and "to meet deadly force with deadly force." You can probably find something akin to the following provision of Florida law (Florida Criminal Code, section 776.031) in the criminal code of your state:

> A person is justified in the use of force ... against another when and to the extent that he reasonably believes that such conduct is necessary to prevent or terminate such other's trespass on, or other tortious or criminal interference with, either real property other than a dwelling or personal property, lawfully in his possession or in the possession of another who is a member of his immediate family or household or of a person whose property he has a legal duty to protect. However, he is justified in the use of deadly force only if he reasonably believes that such force is necessary to prevent the imminent commission of a forcible felony [e.g., aggravated battery, sexual battery, murder, etc.].

If additional problems are posed by the defense of third persons, then those problems are associated with an accentuated likelihood of errors. The following hypothetical situation should illustrate this real concern.

Dianne, a person reasonably believed by law enforcement officials to be one who is often armed and who is engaged in the unlawful sale of various narcotic drugs, was approaching her car, which was parked on a darkened street, when Brent, an undercover police officer, stopped her in his effort to make a lawful arrest. Alert to the risk that Dianne might be armed, Brent had drawn his revolver. As Brent walked toward Dianne, Eric observed the encounter from the window of his home. Reasoning that an armed robbery or even worse was confronting Dianne, Eric grabbed a rifle from a hallway closet, stepped onto his front porch, and fired what proved to be a lethal shot at Brent.

Is Eric's conduct to be excused because he reasonably believed it to be "necessary to prevent the imminent commission of a forcible felony"? In at least a majority of American jurisdictions, Eric's claim that he was exercising his right to come to the defense of others (joined perhaps with a contention that he did what he did because of a reasonable mistake of fact and in an effort to prevent the furtherance of a forcible felony) would probably prevail. Such situations as this, however, do suggest that the risk of error can be substantial when private citizens, albeit in "good faith," use force in coming to the assistance of others. In this hypothetical situation, for instance, Dianne would have enjoyed no special right of any kind to resist Brent if she had reason to believe that he was a law enforcement officer who was involved in the lawful discharge of his legal responsibilities. However, Eric, entirely naive regarding the identity or true conduct of Brent, might well confront no criminal responsibility for his killing of Brent.

Defense of Property

It is a little difficult to imagine a fact situation that would give rise to a "pure" defense of property challenge to a criminal prosecution. Under most circumstances the legal right of citizens to use some appropriate degree of force in their efforts to protect property will be an extension of their right to prevent the commission of a criminal act or to act in the defense of themselves or third parties. However, the general legal theory is that private citizens may lawfully rely on reasonable force in their efforts to protect property from damage, destruction, or loss. Importantly, however, *private citizens almost never enjoy the right to use a type or degree of force that is either intended or likely to be deadly force in the defense of property.*

A classic illustration of the basic principle is provided by the case of *People v. Ceballos*, 12 Cal.3d 470 (1974). His dwelling place having previously been burglarized, Mr. Ceballos connected a .22 caliber rifle to his garage door in such a way that anyone opening that door would discharge the weapon. Two juveniles, Robert and Stephen, who had previously attempted to pry a lock off of the garage door, attempted to enter the garage after the installation of the "spring gun" or "booby trap." Stephen was shot in the face when the door opened. Mr. Ceballos was then charged with and convicted of assault with a deadly weapon. On review by the Supreme Court of California, Mr. Ceballos's conviction was affirmed. Part of the rationale for this holding, of course, was that Mr. Ceballos was not himself in any imminent risk of harm and, instead, that he was merely seeking to protect his property. He thus had no right to rely on what clearly amounted to lethal force.

In the vast majority of all situations, then, citizens may take reasonable steps to protect and defend their property, but those steps must not create a substantial risk of serious bodily injury or death to those who may be involved in criminal conduct. Anyone who steps beyond this line accepts a real risk of a criminal prosecution as well as a civil suit—the initiation of an intentional tort action—by the person to whom they caused harm. On the other hand, the rights of such a citizen would change significantly if an offender were to use deadly force in response to a citizen's lawful efforts to defend property. For instance, were you to make a lawful effort to prevent another person from stealing your automobile and that person then drew a pistol and aimed it at you, then the "rules of the game" would change abruptly. At that point, however, you clearly would be acting primarily in self-defense rather than in defense of your property.

The Defense of Entrapment

The *defense of entrapment* is at best an awkward device that has developed in fairly modern legal history. It is a means by which law enforcement officials (and also persons who are acting on their behalf) are punished for their overly zealous efforts by thwarting their efforts to convict persons whose criminal acts are defined as the direct consequence of what was done by those law enforcement officials. Consequently, defendants may only raise the defense of entrapment if they are contending that the government "manufactured a crime" that would not have been committed had it not been for the opportunity or encouragement its agents provided. In *Sorrells v. United States*, 287 U.S. 435 (1932), for example, the United States Supreme Court observed that entrapment exists "when the criminal design originates with the officials of the Government, and they implant in the mind of an innocent person the disposition to commit the alleged offense and induce its commission in order that they may prosecute." The same basic position has been taken more recently (for example, *Sherman v. United*

States, 356 U.S. 369 [1958]; *Hampton v. United States*, 425 U.S. 484 [1976]).

The scope of the entrapment defense is widely misunderstood. There is no entrapment when the government does no more than provide an opportunity for one who is predisposed to engage in unlawful conduct. For government agents to offer to purchase stolen property, to offer a "bribe" to a public official, to offer to purchase illegal drugs, or to engage in a host of related activities is not to entrap a private citizen. Instead, the question is whether the nature of the government agent's conduct is such that an ordinary citizen who has no predisposition to engage in unlawful conduct might become involved in criminal activities as a direct consequence of the conduct of those government agents. If and only if that question receives an affirmative response, then it is said that the citizen's fundamental right to fair treatment has been violated and that his or her prosecution should not be permitted.

A simple but effective illustration of this is provided by Loewy (1975: 253). He first describes a policeman asking a woman if she will have sex with him for a million dollars. She responds by saying, "Sure thing, I'd do it for two dollars." Is the officer's conduct beyond the limits of what the courts will tolerate? Yes. So substantial an offer might quite easily lure a law-abiding citizen into a criminal act (that is, prostitution). Could she successfully raise entrapment as a defense? It depends. It might well be argued that her response revealed a predisposition to engage in criminal conduct and, therefore, that the woman should be defined as criminally liable. This would be the prevailing legal position today. If, however, one looked at nothing other than the officer's conduct, then the entrapment defense would certainly be successful. However, a narrow focus on the role played by law enforcement agents in the absence of attention to a defendant's predisposition to violate the law has never been adopted by the United States Supreme Court (for instance, *Sherman v. United States*, 356 U.S. 369 [1958]).

The Defense of Insanity

Few ideas are accorded any greater significance in our system of criminal law than is the contention that individuals should only be viewed as criminally liable when their conduct may be thought of as flowing from voluntary choices that have been made by responsible actors. Thus, when a defendant is in a position to contend successfully that the element of either voluntariness or rationality did not characterize his or her behavior, then that defendant is generally not defined as blameworthy. The influential Model Penal Code prepared by the American Law Institute, for example, suggests that "A person is not guilty of an offense unless his liability is based on conduct which includes a voluntary act or the omission to perform an act of which he is physically capable" (Model Penal Code, Section 2.01).

A large number of cases have come before our criminal courts in which defendants have used one or more devices to support their contentions that their conduct lacked the necessary elements of voluntariness or rationality. (Refer back to chapter 2 for our discussion of some of the relevant issues.) A few quick illustrations will have to suffice for our purposes here. In *Government of the Virgin Islands v. Smith*, 278 F.2d 169 (3rd Circuit 1960), for example, the defendant challenged his conviction of two counts of involuntary manslaughter that stemmed from two women having been killed when a car driven by him went out of control and onto a sidewalk. The defendant claimed that he was unconscious at the time of the accident by virtue of his having suffered an epileptic seizure. Jury instructions given by the trial court judge suggested that the defendant had not proven his contention regarding the seizure, but the appellate court held that the defendant had raised sufficient doubt regarding his state of consciousness at the time of the accident and, therefore, that the state had an obligation to prove the voluntariness of the defendant's conduct.

A related if somewhat more bizarre situation was presented by *People v. Newton*, 87 Cal. Rptr. 394 (1970). Newton was convicted of voluntary manslaughter when he shot a police officer after he had himself been seriously wounded. Expert testimony at trial suggested that Newton's claim that he had been unconscious when the shot that killed the policeman was fired might well have been valid. If the shooting had indeed taken place while Newton had neither any understanding of what was taking place nor any ability to voluntarily engage in any form of behavior, then he would have had a sound and complete defense. Thus, the appellate court held that the trial court judge was in error when he failed to instruct the jury about the possible application of unconsciousness as a defense.

Similarly, although voluntary intoxication is seldom if ever a complete defense, those who become involuntarily intoxicated by virtue of mistake, trickery, or coercion are not generally held criminally responsible for any acts (or failures to act) that are shown to be the product of their involuntary intoxication (see, for instance, *People v. Penman*, 110 N.E. 894 [1915] and *Burrows v. State*, 297 P. 1029 [1931]).

Finally, we already have made note of the defense of immaturity and defense of infancy. The ancient common law notion was that very young persons lack the capacity to develop criminal intent and to then voluntarily and with reason translate that intent into blameworthy conduct.

Variations on the sorts of defenses identified above continue to play a significant role in our legal system. Clearly, however, more public and scholarly attention has focused on insanity as a defense and on the closely related contention that defendants, although arguably not meeting the various insanity standards to be addressed below, should not be held fully accountable for their conduct because of their "diminished capacity." Although a thorough discussion of the insanity and the diminished capacity defenses is well beyond the scope of this overview of substantive criminal law, the basic issues and problems they present do warrant comment. (For more exhaustive yet still fairly general treatments, see Fletcher, 1978: 835-845; Inbau et al., 1980: 459-476; Morris, 1982; and Perkins and Boyce, 1982: 950-994.)

Perhaps we should begin our commentary on the insanity defense by emphasizing three exceedingly important points. First, insanity is a purely legal concept and not, as is sometimes thought, a technical concept that has been derived from such fields as medicine, psychiatry, and clinical psychology. To be sure, both prosecutors and defense attorneys routinely seek out "expert witnesses" from whose testimony they seek to establish evidence in support of their respective positions. Legal definitions of who is or is not an "expert," however, tend to be very broad. In Florida, for instance, any person may be qualified as an expert witness on a matter coming before a court if he or she "by knowledge, skill, experience, training, or education may testify about it in the form of an opinion" (Florida Evidence Code, 90.702). Consequently, it is quite common for each "side" to employ its own "hired guns" with the full expectation that those persons will interpret relevant evidence in a fashion that matches the preference of their employer.

Second, insanity defenses have to do with defendants' states of mind at the time of their alleged violation of law. Whereas the state of mind of a defendant is of relevance at multiple points in the criminal justice process (for instance, as it pertains to what motivated a defendant's conduct, as it pertains to the ability of the defendant at the time of trial to assist in his or her own defense, and so on), insanity has only this one referent.

Finally, as a purely practical matter, the vast majority of potential defendants who are perceived by prosecutors and defense attorneys to be obviously and seriously mentally ill are diverted out of the criminal justice system before they confront the jeopardy of a trial. Instead, they confront civil actions aimed at their involuntary commitment to mental health care facilities (see, for instance, Morris, 1982).

The practical as well as the legal problem in these very difficult cases, of course, has to do with whether the conduct of some defendants should be excused because of their state of mind at the time of an otherwise criminal act and, if such excuses are to be accepted, how those excuses are to be evaluated. Here we will comment briefly on four basic standards for evaluating insanity defenses: the so-called *M'Naghten Rule*, the *Irresistible Impulse Test*, the *Substantial Capacity Test*, and the *Direct Product Test*.

The M'Naghten Rule

The roots of the insanity defense may be readily traced to very early English common law developments, and it has been observed that it had become a complete defense by no later than the reign of Edward III (1327-1377) (Perkins and Boyce, 1982: 950). Its modern history, however, is said to have begun with the English trial of Daniel M'Naghten in 1843 (*M'Naghten's Case*, 8 Eng. Rep. 718 [1843]). M'Naghten had killed a man named Edward Drummond because of his incorrect belief that Drummond was Sir Robert Peel, a person whom M'Naghten believed was involved in a plot to kill him. No such plot to kill M'Naghten existed. M'Naghten's attorney contended that his client should not be held criminally responsible for Drummond's death because M'Naghten was insane at the time of the crime.

The so-called *right-wrong test* that was to become the important progeny of this case is not difficult to understand—although it is exceedingly difficult to apply. At its core, the right-wrong test poses a question about the cognitive abilities of defendants at the time of their alleged criminal acts. If, due to some defect of reason caused by "diseases of mind," defendants either (a) were unable to understand and appreciate the nature of their conduct or (b) did not understand that their conduct was wrong, then this test calls for them to be found not guilty by reason of insanity.

At least from a defendant's point of view, the right-wrong test creates a heavy burden. (Prosecutors, on the other hand, have a real fondness for the right-wrong test.) The test often produces the hypothetical illustration of the husband who chokes his wife to death while fully convinced that he is squeezing a lemon. Should such a situation actually materialize, of course, there would be a very high probability that the husband would never be charged with a criminal offense and that he instead would be involuntarily committed for the purpose of treatment.

The Irresistible Impulse and Substantial Capacity Tests

A majority of American jurisdictions adopted the M'Naghten-based right-wrong test. It is certainly not uncommon even today. For example, in the Insanity Defense Reform Act of 1984, Congress defined insanity for the federal jurisdiction in the following fashion:

> It is an affirmative defense to a prosecution under any Federal statute that, at the time of the commission of the acts constituting the offense, the defendant, as a result of severe mental disease or defect, was unable to appreciate the nature and quality or the wrongfulness of his acts. *Mental disease or defect does not otherwise constitute a defense* [emphasis added].

Nevertheless, it soon became apparent that this test had significant and potentially unfair limitations. If, for example, one understands insanity to refer to a condition that has eliminated a defendant's ability to appreciate the wrongfulness of his or her conduct, then one is really suggesting that the defendant is beyond the proper jurisdiction of a criminal court in much the same way as is a young child (who, as we have noted, had the common law right to raise the defense of infancy or immaturity). Insanity, to put the matter a bit differently, would be linked to a determination of whether a criminal court has jurisdiction over a particular person and not to whether some otherwise blame-worthy conduct should be excused. It would appear that the right-wrong test has more to do with jurisdiction than with a legal excuse.

On the other hand, what if one imagined persons who, while understanding that their conduct was indeed unlawful, suffered from some mental disease or disorder that prevented them from controlling themselves? This different image is of persons who encounter such pressures to violate the law that they are in some sense out of control. Responding to such pressures has been viewed by some (for instance, Fletcher, 1978: 836) as being analogous to what we see when defendants raise the defense of necessity or of coercion.

Consider, for example, the wife who returns home a day early from a business trip only to find her husband enjoying the sexual favors being bestowed upon him by a neighbor. Absolutely enraged by her husband's infidelity, she grabs a pistol from a nearby cabinet and shoots both her husband and the neighbor. Did she know what she was doing? Yes. Did she know that what she was doing was wrong? Yes. Would a proper application of the right-wrong test result in her being found not guilty by reason of insanity? No. But should we excuse these two otherwise criminal acts because of the fact that at the time they took place the wife was driven by such a degree of rage and anger? Not so unlike our reaction to the bank teller who turns funds entrusted to him or her to an armed robber, should we conclude that the wife's lethal reaction was, in effect, a consequence of mental pressures she simply could not resist?

Reasonable persons, of course, will respond to this question in a variety of quite different ways. However, such a "crime of passion" serves to illustrate the setting that prompts many jurisdictions to apply what is called an *irresistible impulse test.* It is a test that is often used in conjunction with the right-wrong test. Precisely how the irresistible impulse test is to be applied and evaluated, however, varies widely. At one extreme a defendant might have to show that the strength of the pressure exerted by some mental condition was such that he or she could not have conformed his or her conduct to the requirements of law even if a police officer had been standing at his or her shoulder at the time of the act in question. This very tough standard quite obviously employs the idea of irresistible impulse in an especially literal fashion.

At the other extreme is what is commonly referred to as the *substantial capacity test.* In the Model Penal Code, for example, the following may be found in Section 4.01:

> (1) A person is not responsible for criminal conduct if at the time of such conduct as a result of mental disease or defect he lacks substantial capacity either to appreciate the criminality (wrongfulness) of his conduct or to conform his conduct to the requirement of law.

> (2) As used in this Article, the terms "mental disease or defect" do not include an abnormality manifested only by repeated criminal or otherwise anti-social conduct.

This test is quite obviously far "softer" than is the "police officer at the elbow test" described in the previous paragraph. While key terms in the Model Penal Code definition lack much in terms of precise definitions of their meaning, something closely akin to the Model Penal Code's substantial capacity test may be found in nearly a majority of American jurisdictions.

The Direct Product Test

Finally, we feel obligated to comment briefly on what is usually referred to as the *direct product test.* From the outset, however, it should be noted that the test we will describe has no applicability in any modern American jurisdiction, and is described here purely because of the historical value that some attribute to it.

The direct product test, or "Durham Rule," was derived from a 1954 case that came before the federal circuit court for the District of Columbia (*Durham v. United States,* 214 F.2d 862 [D.C. Circuit 1954]). In *Durham,* Judge David Bazelon sought to breathe a bit of new life into a standard for evaluating insanity defenses that had been advanced many years earlier by a New Hampshire court (*State v. Pike*, 49 N.H. 399 [1870]) but that had been rejected or simply ignored by other jurisdictions. Judge Bazelon's apparent intent was to attribute more significance to developments in the sophistication of the various clinical disciplines. His direct product test thus presented two questions. The first of these had to do with whether the defendant was suffering from a mental disease or defect at the time of his or her conduct. The second question had to do with whether that conduct was the direct product of the mental disease or defect. If the identified mental disease or defect could be linked directly to the conduct of the defendant, then the defendant was to be found not guilty by reason of insanity.

Suffice it to say that virtually nobody was satisfied by the ambiguities that attached to efforts to apply the direct product test. Among its other flaws, the standard provides little guidance regarding what should be taken to be a mental disease or defect or how serious the disease or defect should be before it could be used to provide a legal excuse for otherwise criminal conduct. The doom to which the direct product test seems to have been predestined to meet reached the federal circuit within which it was developed in 1972 (*United States v. Brawner*, 471 F.2d 969 [1972]) and, as we noted earlier, the standard is not in use today in any American jurisdiction.

The Future of the Insanity Defense

Few questions in the area of substantive criminal law present us with more perplexing problems than those we find with the insanity defense. On the one hand, the appeal of everyday life understandings of fairness and justice are such that few of us would wish to impose punishment on any person for an act over which he or she had no control. Thus, we are often inclined to excuse the harm caused by a person who, by reason of some mental disease or defect, either honestly did not know what he or she was doing or who, fully appreciating what he or she was doing, was driven to an act by powerful forces over which he or she had no control. The defense of insanity finds strong support in such feelings and beliefs. On the other hand, the same sorts of attitudes we have about the need for the application of criminal law to be fair and just drive us in an opposite direction when, as is very often the case, evidence used successfully in support of an insanity defense fails to convince us that particular defendants really were insane at the time of their offenses.

The tension that exists between these opposing notions of fairness is greatly elevated by two more or less independent and unfortunate realities when one moves from abstract legal theories of criminal responsibility to the everyday application of criminal law. First, although in theory and sometimes in actual practice the insanity defense can be raised by any defendant and in response to any charged offense, it is generally a defense one encounters only in cases that present the risk of an especially harsh punishment like the death penalty. This is one dimension of the defense that recently prompted Norval Morris (1982: 64) to observe that, "Operationally the defense of insanity is a tribute . . . to our hypocrisy rather than to our morality."

Second, the manner in which trial counsel seek to support or to undermine the insanity defense when it is raised is all too often little more than a mockery of common understandings of justice (see, for instance, Gaylin, 1982). The defense retains "experts" who, to put the matter quite crassly, are paid a fee for telling a story, the obvious object of which is to persuade a judge or a jury that the defendant was surely insane at the time of his or her conduct. The prosecution retains "experts" who are paid a fee for telling a contrary story.

Are those expert physicians, psychiatrists, and clinical psychologists being flatly dishonest? Perhaps. No trial attorney in the nation is likely to be without the names of multiple clinicians who can "tell a good story," a story whose conclusion matches precisely the attorney's preference. But would it really make a difference if each and every clinician were as pure as driven snow? Probably not at all. The relevant facts can be summarized in two sentences: (1) the clinical expertise of "experts" is largely irrelevant to the insanity defense, for it is a legal rather than a clinical concept; and (2) even if clinical opinions were entirely relevant, the simple fact of the matter is that no clinician can do anything more than speculate about a defendant's state of mind at the time of an offense when, as is true in virtually every case, all of that clinician's information was obtained at some point after the offense took place.

These facts, of course, are routinely brushed aside when the insanity defense is actually raised. The consequence is a sort of clinical circus that unfolds in courtrooms all across the country. The outcome of the circus can hardly be said to represent justice, for judges and members of trial court juries are put into an impossible situation. Practically speaking, the outcome of their deliberations will almost necessarily turn on their assessment of which set of clinicians was able to construct the more credible story. That the outcome is often thought to be little more than a farce should shock nobody.

Unfortunately, these problems have no quick or obvious resolution, so the future of the insanity defense remains unclear. Several things, however, deserve consideration. The first of these would call for the total abolition of the special defense of insanity. The odds are strong that such a move would disadvantage neither the state nor the defendant who otherwise would have relied upon the insanity defense. Even today, for example, it is probably true that the vast majority of such defendants are never placed on trial because (1) both the prosecution and the defense agree that they have encountered a mentally ill person who should not be prosecuted, or (2) the defense can argue successfully that the mental condition of these defendants is such that they lack the ability to participate in their own defense and thus cannot be placed on trial. (Naturally, one must remember that defendants who are incompetent to stand trial may be prosecuted later if their mental condition improves sufficiently.)

But what if some number of defendants "slipped between the cracks" created by these two barriers to prosecution and were unable to raise the insanity defense? Indeed, what if prosecutors became more "hard-nosed" after the abolition of the insanity defense and began filing criminal charges against persons whom they previously believed would be found not guilty by reason of insanity?

Again, the problems do not appear to be acute. To begin with, the state would still confront the demand that it prove each material element of an offense and do so "beyond reasonable doubt." As will be discussed in the next section on diminished capacity, a defendant's mental condition is often germane to the state's case. For instance, defendants whose mental state at the time of an offense was such that they did not understand the nature of their conduct, could hardly be convicted on charges that required proof of specific intent (for instance, burglary, many larceny offenses, and so on). Further, the fate of mentally ill defendants is certainly not cast in bronze when they are found to be guilty. There is seldom an automatic sentence that must be imposed (and modifications of mandatory sentence laws could quite easily provide needed flexibility, were the insanity defense to be abolished altogether). Instead, the background and character of defendants—including any indication of mental disease, defect, or disorder—can be, and often is, taken into account before a particular punishment is imposed.

In many ways, then, the perpetual battle that rages between those who advocate the retention or abolition of the insanity defense can be thought of as something of a "tempest in a teapot." Fought purely on a conceptual level, the issues are both real and important. There is nothing trivial about discussions of who ought to be viewed as worthy of punishment. On a practical level, however, it is difficult to understand how the insanity defense serves a purpose that would not be served equally well, were the insanity defense to be abolished. Moreover, the damage that is done to public perceptions of the legitimacy of criminal law by the "clinical circus" described earlier is hardly to be viewed as insignificant.

Diminished Capacity as a Defense

Various facets of *diminished capacity* as a defense have been anticipated in earlier portions of this chapter, so relatively little attention will be devoted to its various forms here. From the very beginning, however, it must be understood that the acceptance of a diminished capacity claim does not excuse a defendant's conduct. Diminished capacity is a partial rather than a complete defense.

In any event, the basic foundation of any diminished capacity defense may be summarized concisely. Because of some abnormal mental or physical condition not sufficient to prove either the insanity of the defendant or that his or her conduct was involuntary, the defendant should be found guilty of a less serious offense than the one charged. Consider the following briefly stated fact situations.

Alexis had been out "drinking with the boys" and had become thoroughly intoxicated when he decided to drive to the apartment complex where he lived. He drove onto the driveway of a home in his neighborhood in the false and drunken belief that it was his own home. When his key failed to fit in the lock of the home's door, he broke a window beside the door, unlocked the door, and entered the home. The owners of the home had observed Alexis' behavior and had called the police. Alexis was arrested while he was in the home and subsequently charged with burglary.

Jean became acutely depressed after she learned that her husband of many years had an inoperable and malignant brain tumor and was under treatment by a psychiatrist for her condition. Day by day her husband's condition deteriorated, and the drugs prescribed for him did progressively little to alleviate his considerable pain and discomfort. One evening he tearfully contended that he simply could not cope with the effects of the disease and begged Jean to administer a lethal dose of the morphine that had been prescribed for him. She walked to the room where the drug was stored, returned to her husband, administered the injection, and called the police when she was confident that he had died. Jean was immediately charged with first-degree murder.

Chuck, a resident of a state within which the insanity defense was defined in terms of a "pure" M'Naghten Rule (that is, the right-wrong test), became enraged when his wife of many years informed him that she was going to file for a divorce so that she would be able to marry a man with whom she had been having an affair. In the heat of the argument that followed, Chuck struck his wife with such force that she fell backwards, hit her head on the edge of a stone fireplace, and died almost immediately. Because of the absence of any apparent premeditation, Chuck was charged with voluntary manslaughter.

What options would be open to you were you to be cast as the defense attorney for Alexis, Jean, or Chuck? Alexis's intoxicated condition obviously contributed to his offensive behavior, but when intoxication is voluntary the intoxicated individual is normally said to be responsible for his or her conduct. Jean was understandably distressed by the plight of her husband, but criminal law does not recognize any hypothetical right of any person to take the life of another even if such a person wishes to die. Indeed, to aid or assist someone who wishes to take his or her own life is generally defined as a criminal offense. Chuck's anger may well have been such that the impulse to strike his wife was one that he honestly could not resist, but the fact that the offense took place in a M'Naghten Rule jurisdiction means that any defense of insanity would be inappropriate. His rage did not eliminate either his ability to distinguish between right and wrong or to appreciate the criminality of his conduct. Does all of this mean that Alexis, Jean, and Chuck should be convicted of the charges brought against them?

The answer can be nothing more than a guarded "perhaps." Often, however, Alexis's voluntary intoxication, Jean's anguish, or Chuck's rage would constitute very different illustrations of what might fall within a broadly defined notion of diminished capacity (for instance, *Fisher v. United States*, 328 U.S. 463 [1946]; *People v. Conley*, 411 P.2d 911 [Cal. 1966]; *People v. Ray*, 533 P.2d 1017 [Cal. 1975]). Our fact situations appear roughly in the order of their likelihood of a diminished capacity defense being successful (Alexis's having the greatest likelihood). Briefly summarized, the rationale for each defense may be stated in the following terms.

First, burglary is most commonly defined as the unlawful entry of a dwelling place with the specific intent to commit a felony offense therein. One might argue that Alexis's drunken condition at the time of his unlawful entry into the dwelling place of another was such that he lacked the ability to develop the specific intent to commit any felony offense within that dwelling place. Although his intoxication would not shield him from guilt on the offense of breaking and entering—a general intent offense—it would often excuse him from offenses for which specific intent is a material element.

Second, first degree murder typically requires proof of malice and premeditation. Used in this context, however, malice does not mean a malicious or hostile attitude toward a victim. It simply means that a person acts with malice aforethought when he or she acts with "wanton disregard for human life" and in a manner that carries with it a high probability that human life will be taken. Jean administered what she fully expected would be a lethal dose of morphine to her husband with the conscious desire to terminate his life. On its face, our description of her conduct clearly reveals both premeditation and malice aforethought. But should the result be a conviction for first-degree murder? It depends. In many jurisdictions the defense counsel would request that the trial jury be instructed that it could return a verdict of guilty on the less serious offense of voluntary manslaughter if it concluded that Jean's extreme anguish and mental condition were such that her diminished capacity was a partial defense.

Finally, while Chuck's diminished capacity defense is fairly obvious, his is perhaps the most difficult of the three hypothetical defendants. In many jurisdictions an insanity defense is an "all-or-nothing" proposition and a diminished capacity defense cannot be used as a "second line of defense" (see, for example, *Fisher v. United States*, 328 U.S. 463 [1946]). Fairly often, however, Chuck's contention that he lacked an ability to control his behavior would reduce the degree of the offense for which he would be convicted from the charge of voluntary manslaughter to involuntary manslaughter.

In effect, then, one may often encounter circumstances that present defendants with no complete defense for their unlawful acts but that do create opportunities for the raising of various partial defenses. Variations on the general theme of diminished capacity defenses serve to illustrate this possibility. These defenses do not serve as complete legal excuses for crimes committed. They do provide a means of reducing the seriousness of the offenses for which defendants are convicted and thereby the harshness of the punishments they are likely to receive.

SUMMARY

In this concluding chapter we have identified and discussed briefly a significant number of common justifications, excuses, and defenses that are raised by defendants who seek to escape conviction altogether (that is, via complete defenses) or to lessen the seriousness of the offenses for which they are convicted (in other words, partial defenses). No useful purpose would be served by a repetition of each of those defenses and their definitions here. Some general principles, however, warrant comment.

Perhaps the general point that deserves attention is that our system of criminal justice, even though it is one within which one can find much deserving harsh criticism, really is one that attributes great significance to the rights of those persons who find themselves confronted with the awesome power of the state and exposed to the considerable risks to life, liberty, and property that come with a criminal prosecution. In principle, if not always in practice, we guard and protect those rights more jealously than do those of any other past or present nation on the face of the earth.

To recognize this lofty set of principles is in no way to excuse abuse, discrimination, and favoritism. In the everyday life of those who make and who apply criminal law we find much that should offend us all. There are laws that protect the interests of the powerful. There are laws that perpetuate the disadvantages of those who are disadvantaged already. There are a host of presumptions and fictions in our body of criminal law that have little to recommend them when they are exposed to the light of reality. There are law enforcement efforts that should shock the conscience of any principled person. There are punishment provisions in our body of criminal law that are brutishly excessive. But should we react to these flaws and inequities by concluding that our system of criminal law is an oppressive sham devoid of legitimacy and not worthy of respect?

We remain convinced that this question deserves a negative—an emphatically negative—response. To say that there are blemishes and warts to be found within any human institution is to say little more than that we recognize that perfection is seldom if ever within the realm of human accomplishment. Humans have the capacity to be petty, to become enraged, to act in a self-serving manner, and to behave against their fellow citizens in horribly discriminatory and harmful ways. Criminal law is sometimes a way they demonstrate all of these negative traits. Yet so, too, do they have the capacity to endorse and steadfastly demand respect for high-minded principles.

Many such principles are pushed into especially sharp relief in our body of criminal and procedural law. If it is true that the quality of a society may be judged by an assessment of the rights and protections that it accords to those who are its least powerful and often its most despised members, then what we have accomplished is hardly insignificant when it is assessed either in absolute or in relative terms. In ways great and small, obvious as well as subtle, those charged with violations of our criminal law routinely and regularly find that the power they enjoy when they are locked in legal combat with the state is greater than that to which they have access in virtually all other areas of their everyday lives. They need not prove their innocence. That is the burden we place on the state. And the burden is not small. We have seen evidence of this throughout this brief monograph. The state must defend the validity of the criminal law it seeks to apply. It must then demonstrate that its law applies both to the charged offense and to the offender it seeks to prosecute. It bears the obligation of proving each and every element of a charged offense by a beyond reasonable doubt standard, and it must overcome contentions raised by defendants who claim that what was done has a legally acceptable justification, defense, or excuse.

Could we have done a better job in fashioning the rules by which we are expected to live and the processes by means of which those rules are translated into everyday practice? Of course. Should we be satisfied with the existing legal status quo? Of course not. Will we do better in years to come? Perhaps. That will depend in large measure on the will and on the principles of ordinary people like us. Today we have a body of criminal and procedural law that is arguably a good deal better than what we deserve. Apathy and fear and a persistent fondness for vengeance will seldom spawn a sound and principled legal system. We have an abundance of each of these negative predispositions. We have always had them. The future of law has always been in doubt.

DISCUSSION QUESTIONS

1. Under what, if any, circumstances should defendants be able to raise insanity as a complete defense? If the defense is to be used, then on the basis of what type(s) of evidence should it be evaluated and, if that evidence is persuasive, what should be done with those who are found to be not guilty by reason of insanity?

2. Ignorance or mistake of law is seldom a satisfactory defense. However, in the United States there are hundreds and hundreds of actions and inactions that are defined as criminal acts and it is obviously inaccurate to assume that each and every citizen is aware of everything that criminal law requires or prohibits. Should an honest and reasonable mistake of law be an acceptable legal excuse? If it were an excuse, how could we evaluate it were it to be raised by defendants?

REFERENCES

AKERS, R. L. and R. HAWKINS [eds.] (1975) Law and Control in Society. Englewood Cliffs, NJ: Prentice Hall.

BAILEY, W. C. (1966) "Correctional outcomes: an evaluation of 100 reports." J. of Criminal Law, Criminology, and Police Sci. (Spring); 153-160.

BASSIOUNI, M. C. (1978) Substantive Criminal Law. Springfield, IL: Charles C Thomas.

BEDAU, H. A. (1978) "Retribution and the theory of punishment." J. of Philosophy 75 (November): 601-620.

———(1984) "Classification-based sentencing: some conceptual and ethical problems." New England J. of Criminal and Civil Confinement 10 (Winter): 1-26.

BEIRNE, P. and R. QUINNEY [eds.] (1982) Marxism and Law. New York: Wiley.

BENTHAM, J. (1975) "The Utilitarian theory of punishment," pp. 25-31 in J. Feinberg and H. Gross (eds.), Punishment. Belmont, CA: Dickenson.

BLACK, D. (1976) The Behavior of Law. New York: Academic Press.

BLACKSTONE, W. (1778) Commentaries on the Laws of England (8th ed.). Oxford: Clarendon.

BOTEIN, S. (1980) Early American Law and Society. New York: Random House.

CAM. H. (1963) Law Finders and Law Makers in Medieval England. New York: Barnes and Noble.

CARDOZO, B. (1924) The Growth of Law. New Haven, CT: Yale Univ. Press.

CASAD, R. C. (1976) Res Judicata. St. Paul: West.

CHAMBLISS, W. and R. SEIDMAN (1982) Law, Order, and Power. Reading, MA: Addison-Wesley.

COHEN, F. (1980) The Law of Deprivation of Liberty. St. Paul: West.

COLLINS, H. (1984) Marxism and the Law. New York: Oxford Univ. Press.

CONRAD, P. and J. W. SCHNEIDER (1980) Deviance and Medicalization: From Badness to Sickness. St. Louis: C. V. Mosby.

CULLEN, F. T. and K. E. GILBERT (1982) Reaffirming Rehabilitation. Cincinnati: Anderson.

DUSTER, T. (1970) The Legislation of Morality: Law, Drugs, and Moral Judgment. New York: Free Press.

FELD, B. C. (1978) "Reference of juvenile offenders for adult prosecution: the legislative alternative to asking unanswerable questions." Minnesota Law R. 62 (April): 515-618.

———(1981) "Juvenile court legislative reform and the serious young offender: dismantling the 'rehabilitative ideal.'" Minnesota Law Rev. 65 (January): 167-242.

———(1983) "Delinquent careers and criminal policy: just deserts and the waiver decision." Criminology 21 (May): 195-212.

FELDBRUGGE, F.J.M. (1966) "Good and bad samaritans: a comparative survey of criminal provisions concerning failure to rescue." Amer. J. of Comparative Law 14, 4: 630-657.

FEINBERG, J. and H. GROSS [eds.] (1975) Punishment: Selected Readings. Belmont, CA: Dickenson.

FLETCHER, G. P. (1971) "Criminal negligence: a comparative analysis." Univ. of Pennsylvania Law Rev. 119 (January): 401-438.

———(1978) Rethinking Criminal Law. Boston: Little, Brown.

FRIEDMAN, L. M. (1975) The Legal System: A Social Sciences Perspective. New York: Russell Sage.

FULLER, L. L. (1964) The Morality of Law. New Haven, CT: Yale Univ. Press.

GARDNER, M. (1953) "Bailey v. Richardson and the Constitution of the United States." Boston Law Rev. 33 (January): 176-193.

GARDNER, T. J. and V. MANIAN (1980) Criminal Law: Principles, Cases and Readings. St. Paul: West.

GAYLIN, W. (1982) The Killing of Bonnie Garland. New York: Simon and Schuster.

GERBER, R. J. and P. D. McAnany [eds.] (1972) Contemporary Punishment: Views, Explanations, and Justifications. Notre Dame, IN: Univ. of Notre Dame Press.

GOLDSTEIN, A. S. (1959) "Conspiracy to defraud the United States." Yale Law J. 68 (January): 405-653.

GREENBERG, D. [ed.] (1981) Crime and Capitalism. Palo Alto, CA: Mayfield.

GROSS, H. (1979) A Theory of Justice. New York: Oxford Univ. Press.

GROSS, H. and A. VON HIRSCH [eds.] (1981) Sentencing. New York: Oxford Univ. Press.

GUSFIELD, J. (1963) Symbolic Crusade: Status Politics and the Temperance Movement. Urbana: Univ. of Illinois Press.

HAGAN, J. (1980) "The legislation of crime and delinquency: a review of theory, method, and research." Law and Society Rev. 14 (Spring): 603-629.

HALL, J. (1960) General Principles of Criminal Law. Indianapolis: Bobbs-Merrill.

———(1963) "Negligent behavior should be excluded from criminal liability." Columbia Law Rev. 63 (April): 632-644.

HALL, J., B. J. GEORGE Jr., and R. FORCE (1976) Criminal Law and Procedure: Cases and Readings. Indianapolis: Bobbs-Merrill.

HAND, L. (1982) "How far is a judge free in rendering a decision," in S. Mermin (ed.), Law and the Legal System. Boston: Little, Brown.

HARPER, R. H. (1904) The Code of Hammurabi, King of Babylon. Chicago: Univ. of Chicago Press.

HART, H.L.A. (1958) "The aims of the criminal law." Law and Contemporary Problems 23 (Summer): 401-441.

———(1961) The Concept of Law. Oxford: Oxford Univ. Press.

———(1968) Punishment and Responsibility: Essays in the Philosophy of Law. Oxford: Oxford Univ. Press.

HOEBEL, E. A. (1954) The Law of Primitive Man: A Study of Comparative Legal Dynamics. Cambridge: Harvard Univ. Press.

HOLMES, O. W. (1881) The Common Law. Boston: Little, Brown.

HYAMS, P. R. (1981) "Trial by ordeal: the key to proof in early common law," pp. 90-126 in M. S. Arnold, T. A. Green, S. A. Scully, and S. D. White (eds.), On the Laws and Customs of England. Chapel Hill: Univ. of North Carolina Press.

INBAU, F. E., J. R. THOMPSON, and J. B. ZAGEL (1980) Criminal Law and Its Administration. Mineola, New York: Foundation.

INGBER, S. (1981) "The Interface of Myth and Practice in Law." Vanderbilt Law Rev. 34 (March): 309-357.

KAIRYS, D. (1982) "Legal reasoning," pp. 11-17 in David Kairys (ed.), The Politics of Law: A Progressive Critique. New York: Pantheon.

KASSEBAUM, G., D. A. WARD and D. M. WILNER (1971) Prison Treatment and Parole Survival. New York: John Wiley.

KEEDY, E. R. (1908) "Ignorance and mistake in the criminal law." Harvard Law Rev. 22 (December): 75-96.

KELSEN, H. (1980) "The Marx-Engels theory of law," pp. 91-104 in W. E. Evan (ed.), The Sociology of Law: A Social-Structural Perspective. New York: Free Press.

KEMPIN, F. G. (1973) Historical Introduction to Anglo-American Law in a Nutshell. St. Paul: West.

KINNANE, C. H. (1952) Anglo American Law. Indianapolis: Bobbs-Merrill.

KORN, R. R. and L. W. MCCORKLE (1959) Criminology and Penology New York: Holt, Rinehart and Winston.

KRISBERG, B. and J. AUSTIN (1978) The Children of Ishmael: Critical Perspectives on Juvenile Justice. Palo Alto, CA: Mayfield.

LAFAVE, W. R. and A. W. SCOTT (1972) Handbook on Criminal Law. St. Paul: West.

LERMAN, P. (1975) Community Treatment and Social Control: A Critical Analysis of Juvenile Correctional Policy. Chicago: Univ. of Chicago Press.

LIPTON, D., R. MARTINSON, and J. WILKS (1975) The Effectiveness of Correctional Treatment: A Survey of Treatment Evaluation Studies. New York: Praeger.

LOEWY, A. H. (1975) Criminal Law. St. Paul: West.

MACAULAY and other Indian Law Commissioners (1851) A Copy of the Penal Code Prepared by the Indian Law Commissioners. London: Austin.

MARX, K. and F. ENGELS (1973) Marx/Engels Selected Works, Vol. I. Moscow: Progress.

MCNAMARA, R. B. (1982) Constitutional Limitations on Criminal Procedure. Colorado Springs: Shepard's/McGraw-Hill.

MENNINGER, K. (1968) The Crime of Punishment. New York: Viking.

MERMIN, S. (1982) Law and the Legal System. Boston: Little, Brown.

MIX, D. D. (1968) "The misdemeanor approach to pollution control." Arizona Law Rev. 10 (Summer): 90-96.

MORRIS, N. (1974) The Future of Imprisonment. Chicago: Univ. of Chicago Press.

———(1982) Madness and the Criminal Law. Chicago: Univ. of Chicago Press.

MUELLER, G.O.W. (1955) "Mens rea and the law without it." West Virginia Law Rev. 58 (December): 34-68.

MURPHY, J. G. [ed.] (1985) Punishment and Rehabilitation. Belmont, CA: Wadsworth.

PACKER, H. (1962) "Mens rea and the Supreme Court," pp. 107-124 in P. B. Jurland (ed.), The Supreme Court Review. Chicago: Univ. of Chicago Press.

———(1968) The Limits of the Criminal Sanction. Stanford: Stanford Univ. Press.

PARK, R. (1978) Classroom lecture quoted in E. H. Sutherland and D. R. Cressey, Criminology, 10th edition. Philadelphia: Lippincott.

PERKINS, R. M. (1969) Criminal Law. Mineola, NY: Foundation.

PERKINS, R. M. and R. N. BOYCE (1982) Criminal Law. Mineola, NY: Foundation.

PINCOFFS, E. L. (1966) The Rationale of Legal Punishment. New York: Humanities Press.

PLOSCOWE, M. (1939) Crime and Criminal Law. New York: Collier and Son.

POLLOCK, SIR FREDERICK and F. W. MAITLAND (1895) History of English Law (vol. 1). Cambridge: The Univ. of Cambridge Press.

POUND, R. (1921) The Spirit of the Common Law. Boston: Little, Brown.

———(1939) The History and System of the Common Law. New York: Collier and Son.

RIEDEL, M. and T. P. THORNBERRY (1978) "The effectiveness of correctional programs: an assessment of the field," pp. 418-432 in B. Krisberg and J. Austin (eds.), The Children of Ishmael. Palo Alto, CA: Mayfield.

SABINE, G. H. and T. L. THORSON (1973) A History of Political Theory. Hinsdale, IL: Dryden.

SCHWARTZ, H. (1976) Justice by the Book: Aspects of Jewish and American Law. New York: Women's League for Conservation Judaism.

SEAGLE, W. (1941) The Quest for Law. New York: Knopf.

SIMPSON, A.W.B. (1981) "The laws of Ethelbert," pp. 3-17 in M. S. Arnold et al. (eds.), On the Law and Customs of England. Chapel Hill: Univ. of North Carolina Press.

SMITH, M. (1956) "Elements of law," pp. 171-378 in A. T. Vanderbilt (ed.), Studying Law. New York: New York Univ. Press.

TAPPAN, P. W. (1960) Crime, Justice and Correction. New York: McGraw-Hill.

THOMAS, C. W. (1986) Corrections in America. Beverly Hills, CA: Sage.

———and J. R. HEPBURN (1983) Criminal, Criminal Law, and Criminology. Dubuque, IA: William C. Brown.

THOMAS, C. W. and D. M. BISHOP (forthcoming) "The impact of legal sanctions on delinquency: an assessment of the utility of labeling and deterrence theory." J. of Criminal Law and Criminology.

THOMAS, C. W. and S. BILCHIK (forthcoming) "Prosecuting juveniles in criminal courts: a legal and an empirical analysis." J. of Criminal Law and Criminology.

THOMPSON, E. P. (1982) "The rule of law," pp. 130-137 in P. Beirne and R. Quinney (eds.), Marxism and Law. New York: Wiley.

WADLINGTON, W., C. H. WHITEBREAD, and S. M. DAVIS (1983) Cases and Materials on Children in the Legal System. Mineola, NY: Foundation.

WASSERSTROM, R. (1960) "Strict liability in the criminal law." Stanford Law Rev. 12 (July): 731-745.

WEBER, M. (1954) Law in Economy and Society. Translated by E. Shils and M. Rheinstein. Cambridge: Harvard Univ. Press.

WILLIAMS, G. L. (1961) Criminal Law: The General Part 2, 2nd edition. London: Stevens.

WOLFGANG, M. E. and M. REIDEL (1973) "Race, judicial discretion, and the death penalty." The Annals of the Amer. Academy of Pol. and Soc. Sci. 407 (May). 119-133.

CASE LAW

Allen v. McCurry, 449 U.S. 90 (1980).
Ashe v. Swenson, 397 U.S. 453 (1970).
Bailey v. State, 22 Ala. App. 185 (1927).
Barker v. Wingo, 407 U.S. 514 (1972).
Bartkus v. Illinois, 359 U.S. 121 (1959).
Benton v. Maryland, 395 U.S. 784 (1969).
Blackledge v. Perry, 417 U.S. 21 (1974).
Blockburger v. United States, 284 U.S. 299 (1932).
Bloom v. Richards, 2 Ohio 387 (1853).
Bouie v. City of Columbia, 378 U.S. 347 (1964).
Brown v. Board of Education of Topeka, 347 U.S. 483 (1954).
Brown v. Ohio, 432 U.S. 161 (1977).
Bullington v. Missouri, 451 U.S. 430 (1980).
Burrows v. State, 297 p. 1029 (1931).
Bush v. Commonwealth, 78 Ky. 268 (1880).
Calder v. Bull, 3 U.S. (3 Dall.) 386 (1798).
Commonwealth v. Chapman, 54 Mass. 68 (1849).
Commonwealth v. Hackett, 84 Mass. 136 (1861).

Commonwealth v. Koczwara, 395 Pa. 575 (1959).
Commonwealth v. McManus, 282 Pa. 25 (1925).
Commonwealth v. Pierce, 138 Mass. 165 (1884).
Commonwealth v. Wright, 455 Pa. 480 (1974).
Connally v. General Construction Company, 269 U.S. 385 (1926).
Counselman v. Hitchcock, 142 U.S. 547 (1892).
Cornell v. State, 159 Fla. 687 (1947).
Crews v. State, 44 Ga. App. 546 (1932).
Crist v. Bretz, 437 U.S. 28 (1978).
Curtis v. State, 118 Ala. 125 (1897).
Dillingham v. United States, 423 U.S. 64 (1975).
Donnelly v. DeChristoforo, 416 U.S. 637 (1974).
Durham v. United States, 214 F.2d 862 (D.C. Circuit 1954).
Dusky v. United States, 362 U.S. 402 (1960).
Eisenstadt v. Baird, 405 U.S. 438 (1972).
Fisher v. United States, 328 U.S. 463 (1946).
Gooding v. Wilson, 405 U.S. 518 (1972).
Government of the Virgin Islands v. Smith, 278 F. 2d 169 (3rd Circuit 1960).
Grayned v. City of Rockford, 408 U.S. 104 (1972).
Green v. United States, 355 U.S. 184 (1957).
Griffin v. California, 380 U.S. 609 (1965).
Hampton v. United States, 425 U.S. 484 (1976).
Harris v. Washington, 404 U.S. 55 (1971).
Harris v. Commonwealth, 79 Va. 374 (1884).
Heath v. Alabama, (Dockett No. 84-5555 argued 10-9-85).
In re Marley, 29 Cal. 2d 525 (1946).
Johnson v. State, 64 Fla. 321 (1912).
Jones v. State, 220 Ind. 384 (1942).
Jones v. United States, 113 U.S. App. D.C. 352 (D.C. Cir. 1962).
Kastigar v. United States, 406 U.S. 441 (1971), (1972).
Klopfer v. North Carolina, 386 U.S. 213 (1967).
Lambert v. California, 355 U.S. 225 (1957).
Lanzetta v. New Jersey, 306 U.S. 451 (1939).
Letner v. State, 156 Tenn. 68 (1927).
Lewis v. Commonwealth, 19 Ky. L. Rep. 1139 (1897).
Loving v. Virginia, 388 U.S. 1 (1967).
Malloy v. Hogan, 378 U.S. 1 (1964).
Marbury v. Madison, 5 U.S. 137 (1803).
Marks v. United States, 430 U.S. 191 (1977).
McBoyle v. United States, 283 U.S. 25 (1931).
McCutcheon v. State, 199 Ind. 247 (1927).
McDaniel v. State, 76 Ala. 1 (1884).
McLaughlin v. Florida, 379 U.S. 184 (1964).
Michael M. v. Superior Court, 450 U.S. 464 (1981).
M'Naghten's Case, 8 Eng. Rep. 718 (1843).
Montana v. United States, 440 U.S. 147 (1979).
Morey v. Commonwealth, 108 Mass. 433 (1871).
Morrisette v. United States, 342 U.S. 246 (1952).
North Carolina v. Pearce, 395 U.S. 711 (1969).

O'Callahan v. Parker, 395 U.S. 258 (1969).
Ogden v. Saunders, 25 U.S. (12 Wheat) 286 (1827).
Papachristou v. City of Jacksonville, 405 U.S. 156 (1972).
Parsons v. State, 21 Ala. 300 (1852).
Peck v. Dunn, 574 P.2d 367 (Utah 1978).
People v. Cabaltero, 31 Cal. App. 2d (1939).
People v. Ceballos, 12 Cal.3d 470 (1974).
People v. Conley, 411 P.2d 911 (Cal. 1966).
People v. Cook, 39 Mich. 236 (1878).
People v. Decina, 2 N.Y. 2d, 133 (1956).
People v. Fowler, 178 Cal. 657 (1918).
People v. Henderson, 19 Cal. 3d 86 (1977).
People v. Hickman, 59 Ill. 2d 89 (1974).
People v. Lewis, 124 Cal. 551 (1899).
People v. Newton, 87 Cal. Rptr. 394 (1970).
People v. Pavlic, 227 Mich. 562 (1924).
People v. Penman, 110 N.E. 894 (1915).
People v. Ray, 553 P.2d 1017 (Cal. 1975).
People v. Stamp, 2 Cal. App. 3d 203 (1970).
Petite v. United States, 361 U.S. 529 (1960).
Powell v. Texas, 392 U.S. 514 (1968).
Reed v. Reed, 404 U.S. 71 (1971).
Regina v. Dudley and Stephens, 14 Q.B.D. 273 (1884).
Regina v. Faulkner, 13 Cox C.C. 550 (1877).
Regina v. Instan, 1 Q.B. 450 (1893).
Regina v. Nicholls, 13 Cox C.C. 75 (1874).
Rex v. Jordan, 40 Crim. App. 152 (1956).
Robinson v. California, 370 U.S. 660 (1962).
Roe v. Wade, 410 U.S. 113 (1972).
Serfass v. United States, 420 U.S. 377 (1975).
Sherman v. United States, 356 U.S. 369 (1958).
Simpson v. Wainwright, 439 F.2d 948 (5th Cir. 1971).
Smith v. Goguen, 415 U.S. 566 (1974).
Sorrells v. United States, 287 U.S. 435 (1932).
State v. Arizona Mines Supply Co., 107 Ariz. 199 (1971).
State v. Cooper, 180 Mont. 68 (1979).
State v. Edgerton, 100 Iowa 63 (1896).
State v. Gilmore, 320 Ill. 233 (1926).
State v. Glover, 330 Mo. 709 (1932).
State v. Johnson, 36 Del. 341 (1934).
State v. McKeiver, 213 A. 2d 320 (1965).
State v. Morphy, 33 Iowa 270 (1871).
State v. Pike, 49 N.H. 399 (1870).
State v. Rueckert, 221 Kan. 727 (1977).
State v. Scates, 50 N.C. 420 (1858).
State v. Wood, 53 Vt. 1560 (1881).
Stephenson v. State, 205 Ind. 141 (1932).
Thomas v. State, 139 Ala. 80 (1904).
Toussie v. United States, 397 U.S. 112 (1970).

INDEX

ABOUT THE AUTHORS

CHARLES W. THOMAS is a Professor of Criminology and Sociology at the University of Florida as well as the Director of the University of Florida's Center for Studies in Criminology and Law. His work has appeared in such research journals as the *American Criminal Law Review, Criminology, Crime and Delinquency, Journal of Criminal Law and Criminology,* and *Social Problems.* His book-length publications include *Crime, Criminal Law, and Criminology,* a widely adopted textbook which he co-authored with John R. Hepburn. Professor Thomas's present research interests include research on recent developments in juvenile law and the role played by Eighth Amendment challenges to capital punishment.

DONNA M. BISHOP is a Senior Research Associate in the Center for Studies in Criminology and Law at the University of Florida. With special interests in criminal procedure, criminological theory, and juvenile delinquency, examples of her research have appeared in *Criminology,* the *Justice Quarterly,* the *Journal of Criminal Law and Criminology,* and *Social Forces.* Much of her ongoing research focuses on the operation of various facets of the juvenile system, especially procedures which permit some types of juvenile offenders to be prosecuted in criminal courts.